MW00366038

EDUCATION OF
A KABBALIST

KABBALIST RAV BERG

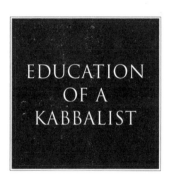

EDUCATION
OF A
KABBALIST

KABBALIST RAV BERG

FOR MY WIFE

 AREN

IN THE VASTNESS OF TIME,
AND THE INFINITY OF SPACE,
IT IS MY GREAT BLISS AND
MY MOST TREASURED GIFT
TO SHARE A SOULMATE
WITH YOU.

For further information:
The Kabbalah Centre™
Director Rav Berg

1-800-KABBALAH™
www.kabbalah.com™
14 Ben Ami St., Tel Aviv, Israel 63342
155 E. 48th, New York City, NY 10017
1062 S. Robertson Blvd., Los Angeles, CA 90035

First Edition
September 2000
Printed in Canada

ISBN 1-57189-146-3

May the Light that shines
through the lineage of Kabbalists
Open the heart of all people to come closer
to the Light of The Creator.
May it bring peace, love and harmony
between all mankind.

———•◆•———

Nissim ben Yitzchak and Kamuna
Devorah bat Machluf and Perla
Rachel, Sarah, Esther and Miriam
daughters of Nissim and Devorah

EDUCATION OF A KABBALIST:

PROLOGUE

If you pick up this book with some of the common misconceptions about Kabbalah, you will encounter a number of surprises and unexpected revelations. If you imagine a Kabbalisitic rabbi to be a reclusive mystic isolated from the everyday world, or that Kabbalah is an inventory of secret rites and rituals with access granted to only a few, you will be relieved of these notions. The biggest surprise of all, however, may well be this: Although the book is entitled *Education of a Kabbalist*, with Rav Berg as author, on each page and almost in every sentence, Rav Berg focuses our attention on Rabbi Yehuda Brandwein, his teacher, mentor, and Kabbalistic master.

How are we to understand this seemingly curious deflection of interest from the supposed subject of the book, which is the education of Rav Berg himself?

The truth is, however, Education of a Kabbalist could have been written in no other way. If Rav Berg had explicitly drawn our attention to himself, the book would have been a contradiction in terms. It is a defining attribute of a Kabbalist to have moved beyond the realm of ego in any form. Were Rav Berg's ego a presence in these pages, the book's own thesis would have been subverted: In that case, clearly, the author could not be a Kabbalist, let alone an educated one.

What readers should understand, therefore, is that Rav Berg's depiction of Rabbi Brandwein presents not just one individual, but an extraordinary line of souls, including, by implication, Rav Berg's own, who have achieved a truly wondrous level of elevation. This is what the term Kabbalist really means. Although he literally would not say this directly about himself, this is what Rav Berg really is.

When someone merits the title of Kabbalist, this denotes four specific personal qualities and scholarly attainments. To grasp this, one must first understand the schematic representation of physical and spiritual reality which Kabbalah calls the *Ten Sfirot* or *Tree of Life*. This is a sequence of ten levels of energy that begins with the physical world, and reaches completion with the Creator Himself. It is the great task of every soul to climb this ladder though it may entail much suffering and numerous setbacks and even many lifetimes. Within this system, a Kabbalist is first and foremost, a person who has advanced much further than an average person along the ten ascending levels of illumination. This does not mean that a Kabbalist lives in a different world than the rest of us, but that he lives in many different worlds at the same time. His consciousness is here with us, but is also somewhere above us. Rabbi Brandwein, for example, lived like many of us, taking buses, dealing with financial matters, and working in a blue-collar industry. Even so, his soul was "in the world, but not of it." He was someone who experienced both the ultimate and the relative dimensions at one and the same instant. Many spiritual traditions refer to this genuinely transcendant category of being, but never has the flesh-and-blood presence of such a person been more clearly felt than in these pages.

A second defining quality of a Kabbalist is his living every day and every moment according to the teachings of Kabbalah. A Kabbalist observes the rituals, recites the prayers, and follows the precepts. This means not only understanding Kabbalah on an intellectual level and feeling its spiritual power at the depth of one's being, but also using the tools of Kabbalah to draw closer to the Creator. Over the past hundred years, a number of writers have achieved a superb grasp of Kabbalah on a scholarly level. Together, Walter Benjamin, Raphael Patai, and Gershom Scholem may have learned as much about the tradition as it is possible to learn. But learning about Kabbalah is something very different from living it. We too can learn a great deal about Kabbalah by reading the works of Gershom Scholem, and it might require many years to traverse those complex volumes. But we can come to know more about Kabbalah simply by connecting to one Shabbat with our whole hearts.

Thirdly, a Kabbalist does not live in the tradition alone. He is deeply committed to teaching Kabbalah, to spreading the wisdom of Kabbalah to all who have a desire to learn, and to reawakening spirituality even in those who are deeply estranged from this dimension of themselves. Again and again in these pages, we see Rabbi Brandwein and Rav Berg printing, publishing, and distributing the great works of Kabbalah, most notably those of Rabbi Yehuda Ashlag, who was the founder of the Kabbalah Centre in Jerusalem and who had been Rabbi Brandwein's teacher.

Kabbalah, especially at this point in history, is not intended to be the private domain of anyone. Kabbalists are no longer like medieval alchemists, sequestered in a locked room and pondering arcane knowledge in solitude. In fact, the present truth is quite the opposite. The doors of that room have been unlocked by the Kabbalists themselves, and the long-hidden wisdom has been brought out into the world. No one, not even Rabbi Brandwein himself, has better exemplified this aspect of a Kabbalist than Rav Berg. Millions of people have discovered Kabbalah because of his work. Tens of millions of books have been printed. Through writing, publishing, and as a living example, Rav Berg has introduced Kabbalah to humanity as a whole through 39 established Centres worldwide.

The fourth and final attribute of a Kabbalist is the most pertinent to this memoir. A Kabbalist is someone who has *received* a heritage of teachings and wisdom from a master, who in turn received it from a still earlier master, throughout the ages in a great unbroken chain reaching back to Abraham the Patriarch. Just as Kabbalah teaches that time and space have no reality outside the physical world, the individual identities of the great Kabbalists are distinct but also irrelevant. They are an upward spiral of spiritual energy, not merely a list of names and dates.

It is through this lens we must see clearly that when Rav Berg speaks of Rabbi Brandwein, he is also speaking of himself: Rav Berg's own identity as a holographic expression of the great Kabbalists, and even of Kabbalah itself. Every piece of a hologram contains the entire image, but from an angle that differs ever so slightly from any other fragment. In the same way, every true Kabbalist teaches us the same timeless wisdom, but each offers a perspective uniquely appropriate to the historical setting and spiritual needs of the time in which he lives. As the new millennium begins, and with it, the great transformations that Kabbalah has predicted over the centuries, Rav Berg is not only the messenger, but the personification of Kabbalah for our time. His humility and self-effacing persona in this volume is not a contradiction of his importance as a Kabbalist, but rather proof of it.

Let us read *Education of a Kabbalist* to enlighten ourselves about how a pure soul conducts itself in this world and, to the extent of our ability, try to live a more soul-filled life.

INTRODUCTION

When I first visited Israel in the spring of 1964, I had no clear intention to study Kabbalah, but through a series of fortunate coincidences, I was introduced to Rabbi Brandwein. As a result, I became a student of a man whom I believe was the greatest Kabbalist of his time. That this should happen to me was highly paradoxical. It was both surprising and not surprising. In the United States, I had been trained as a conventional rabbi, but because of traditional religion's lack of inclusiveness and its inability to provide practical answers to life's real problems, I also engaged in a business career. Yet only a few years after meeting Rabbi Brandwein, I had dedicated myself to bringing the wisdom of Kabbalah to all people. This was the effect Rabbi Brandwein had on everyone—and the effect also of Kabbalah, which I first learned through him. He was, as I came to learn, uniquely gifted in his ability to draw back those who had become alienated, to impart his spirituality to all who met him, and to unfold the truths of The Creator.

In some ways, my story is unique, but in other respects many people have taken a similar journey. Like most children, I had been deeply moved by spirituality, and had received the intensely religious education of my culture. Later, I studied for the

Rabbinate, only to become profoundly disillusioned by my religion as it had been taught to me. By the time I arrived in Tel Aviv in the Spring of 1964, I thought I was simply looking for a respite from the business world. On a deeper level, however, I believe that the spiritual self within me was coming back to life. Privately, I had never forsaken my religion, and now I again became eager for a more public expression of it. I had known for several years that a distant relative of mine now living in Israel, Rabbi Yehuda Brandwein, was a well-known Kabbalist. The curiosity of my younger self was quickly reawakened, and I set about to meet him. It was not long after that first meeting that I took a leave of absence from my business to study with Rabbi Brandwein full-time.

What follows is a memoir which is told as much for Rabbi Brandwein's insights and knowledge of Kabbalah as it is to relate the story of my own spiritual development. Much of Kabbalah you will read here was taught to Rabbi Brandwein by his own teacher, Rabbi Yehuda Halevy Ashlag—and to Rabbi Ashlag by his teacher before him, and so on back through the great and honorable lineage of the Kabbalistic tradition.

This book is organized loosely in chronological fashion, but in Kabbalah, chronology is always less important than the deeper forms of truth. You are encouraged to read this book any way you like—from start to finish—or randomly, one story at a time. If you find some of the ideas difficult to understand, this is to be expected. Truth is not always easily grasped, but if the word of The Creator is precious to you, if you yearn to flow after the Light of The Creator and His beneficence, understanding will be achieved.

May I forever merit to deserve the blessed wisdom of my teacher, and the Light of Kabbalah which shines through his blessed soul.

"HE IS NOT A RABBI, HE IS A KABBALIST"

Rabbi Yehuda Tzvi Brandwein was born in the city of Safed, in what is now Israel, in 1904. He began studying Kabbalah as a child, preparing to carry on a long tradition of teachers in his family. His own teacher was Rabbi Yehuda Ashlag, probably the most important Kabbalist of the early 20th century.

When I met Rabbi Brandwein I did not know the details of his life and education, but I did know that something deep inside me had been re-awakened. At once, I felt drawn to study with him, and it was my enormous good fortune that he agreed. Again and again over the years, I saw his ability to touch those who had become alienated from traditional religion—and I myself was a prime example.

The terms of my study were quite straightforward. I helped with the daily tasks of the Kabbalah Centre in Jerusalem, which had been established by Rabbi Ashlag in 1922. I also accompanied Rabbi Brandwein in his work as chief Rabbi of the Histadrut—the Israeli Workers Union, which had thousands of members — and devoted as much time as possible to reading the sacred texts of Kabbalah.

Each evening, I spoke with the Rabbi about

what I had learned that day. Sometimes he responded with a question or a brief comment, but more often he simply nodded to acknowledge that I understood. Kabbalah is unique in its emphasis on formal study of the sacred texts—not only as the way of elevating our individual souls, but also to hasten the redemption of all humanity. Each of our actions in the everyday world, even the most trivial, has consequences far beyond the boundaries of our own lives, but study is especially important in this respect. The *Zohar* even asserts that the continuing exile of the "chosen people" results from failure to study diligently enough. Conversely, studying with humility, concentration, and in the proper setting—especially late at night— is not simply an opportunity to learn Kabbalah: It is moving the entire world closer to immortality.

Of course, on Shabbat we rested, for as it is written in the Midrash, "If Israel keeps one Shabbat as it should be kept, the Messiah will surely come."

At this point, it's important to clarify Kabbalah's concept of the Messiah. Although *Messiah* is commonly understood to mean a single individual who will someday appear and bring about the redemption of the world, Kabbalah teaches that humanity itself is the true Messiah. When humanity achieves a level of spirituality that merits our redemption, that redemption will have already been realized by the spiritual transformation that has taken place. When there are enough spiritually worthy people—those who keep Shabbat as it should be kept, for example—the Messiah will indeed be here. The Messiah, therefore, is already present as a spiritual potential in each of our hearts; our task is first to recognize that potential, and then to actualize it through the tools that the Creator has provided.

Kabbalah teaches that Shabbat and the other holy days are opportunities to connect with the Light of the Creator in unique and powerful ways. Yet Rabbi Brandwein was well aware of the lack of spiritual awareness in Israel, and indeed throughout the world. It caused him great pain when people failed to use the spiritual tools the Creator had provided.

Not long after my joining the Kabbalah Centre, I saw a dramatic instance of Rabbi Brandwein's power to touch people on a spiritual level. It was in Haifa, on a Shabbat morning in the early spring. The weather was very clear with hardly a cloud in the sky. We were approaching the main square of the city, when we saw a tall, well-dressed man walking toward us. He was smiling and smoking a cigarette.

"That is Mr. Aba Chushi," Rabbi Brandwein said to me. "He's the Mayor of Haifa."

As Aba Chushi greeted us, he and Rabbi Brandwein had a brief, pleasant conversation. Then they wished each other Shabbat Shalom, and we continued on our way.

Later, we returned to Haifa, and I accompanied the Rabbi on a visit to the Mayor. Again, their relations seemed quite cordial, and the Mayor had set a gracious meal for us to enjoy. Half-way through our lunch, however, Mr. Chushi set down his fork.

"I must tell you, Rabbi. You have had a strong influence on my life."

This seemed surprising to me since I knew the Rabbi rarely traveled to Haifa and he did not know the Mayor particularly well.

"Do you remember when we met last month on Shabbat?" Mr. Chushi asked.

My teacher smiled, "Of course."

"When we met, if you recall, I was smoking, and now I have given it up."

My teacher did not say, Good! I'm glad you've stopped smoking on Shabbat, as all proper religious people should. He only asked why.

"Frankly, it was because I saw the pain on your face that I was smoking on Shabbat. I felt immediately your deep concern for me. And do you know, since I stopped I have gone to my doctor, and he has told me it was a very lucky thing that I did."

"I am happy for you," the Rabbi said. "Happy that you will now know the joy of Shabbat, and of course glad about your health as well." Then he told us something I have never forgotten, and I doubt if Mr. Chushi has either. In the *Zohar*, Shabbat is called a time when the entire arrangement of the order of the worlds is changed. Light descends like dew from the upper to the lower worlds and from there Divine abundance flows to all of Creation.

"So you see," he finished. "Your doctor was right. You are a very lucky man."

Beyond doubt, something in the tone of his voice showed that this was a wise and learned man speaking. Moreover, this was a Kabbalist—and the most important purpose of this book is to make clear exactly what that means. Not just to tell about Rabbi Brandwein, but to show how he conducted himself day by day in the real world. For a Kabbalist practices Kabbalah not only during prayers in the sanctuary, but in literally everything he does.

I was sometimes asked why I had chosen Rabbi

Brandwein as my teacher, and it was difficult to give a precise answer, except to say that I was drawn to him by a power that was impossible to deny. The secretary of the Histadrut, a Mr. Levi, was frequently asked a similar question. Why had he chosen Rabbi Brandwein to be the chief rabbi of the Workers' Union? Clearly, the union members were estranged from any deep spirituality. They went out dancing on religious holidays, nor did they observe any of the traditions. Wouldn't a more assimilated rabbi would have been more acceptable?

Mr. Levi always replied that Rabbi Brandwein was not just a rabbi, but that he was a Kabbalist, and that made all the difference. I was beginning my studies at the time, and I did not fully understand the full meaning of Mr. Levi's answer. But that meaning became clearer and more powerful for me every day.

"DO NOT LOOK AT THE CONTAINER, BUT AT WHAT IS WITHIN"

"What is lacking really in the world," Rabbi Brandwein sometimes said, "is love for others." It was during a trip with him to a kibbutz, in 1964, that I came to understand what this really meant.

When we set out on this trip I had only been

in Israel a few months, and had never visited a kibbutz. Rabbi Brandwein told me that the one we
were visiting, in Ein Gedi, was not a religious place
at all. The people were hard workers, but freely
admitted they were not very spiritual.

My upbringing had trained me to categorize
people—some were worthy of attention, others
were not. Why, I wondered, were we taking the time
to visit this place? Surely other people were more
deserving of my teacher's wisdom. Why would
someone with the gifts of Rabbi Brandwein want to
even associate with such people?

As we arrived at the kibbutz, the kibbutz secretary ran up to Rabbi Brandwein and the two
embraced like long-lost brothers. I was amazed. The
secretary was dressed in very ragged work clothes,
his background was completely different from Rabbi
Brandwein's, and to my knowledge they shared no
spiritual bond. I kept asking myself, 'What could
these two people possibly have in common? What
connection is there between them? Why is my
teacher even here?'

Then I got a real shock. The kibbutz secretary
led us into the kitchen of the compound, where he
proudly told us that he had carried out all my
teacher's instructions regarding the koshering of the

kitchen. As Rabbi Brandwein carefully inspected the kitchen, the secretary's face beamed with joy. Then I understood what I should have all along: My teacher had brought faith and spirituality to this kibbutz, and he had done it with love.

For someone unfamiliar with the factions and fragmentation that characterize life in Israel, it may be difficult to grasp how astonishing this really was. That the secretary of a thoroughly secular kibbutz would create a kosher kitchen—this was completely unheard of. For me, the sensation was like seeing someone using a foreign language that seemed totally unconnected to his appearance—as if a Swedish farmer had suddenly begun speaking fluent Chinese. But, as always when I was with Rabbi Brandwein, there was a Kabbalistic lesson to be learned: What is concealed is always more powerful than what is revealed, whether it's the feelings in a man's heart beneath his ragged clothes or the hidden meaning within a Biblical passage.

Over the years, I have come to understand that these types of experiences were the norm for Rabbi Brandwein. Because of his study of Kabbalah he was able to approach almost anyone, and this was one of his great strengths. He could draw a person to spirituality without force or insistence of any kind. Indeed, this was as his own teacher, Rabbi Ashlag, had instructed him, "There is no coercion in spirituality." This is a very important principle. If people are unprepared to move forward spiritually, coercing them to do so can actually be destructive.

In Kabbalah, this idea is expressed through the primordial narrative often referred to as *the Light and the Vessel*. Before the Creation of the world, in fact, before the Creation of the universe itself, the love and beneficence of the Creator was the only reality. Kabbalah refers to this divine energy, love and beneficence as the Light. It is tempting to say that the Light was "everywhere and at every moment," though time and space as we know them had not yet come into being. In order to fully express its inherent nature to give and to share, the Light brought into being a receiving principle, the Vessel. As the Vessel received more and more Light, it gradually manifested a sharing intention of its own. Although it is an oversimplification to speak of these primal energies in human terms, one could say that the Vessel wanted to be more like the Light.

The Vessel therefore "pushed back" the Light. It no longer wished to receive unearned benevolence. It desired to give and to share on its own. However, like an adolescent child who runs away from home and then quickly wants to come back again, the Vessel soon desired the return of the Light, despite the fact that it was no longer capable of allowing the Light in without internal conflict or pain. When the Light returned in full force, the Vessel simply shattered. "Too much of a good thing" proved catastrophic.

The concept of the shattering of the Vessel is a powerful convergence of Kabbalah and the modern science's Big Bang theory of Creation. As in the Big Bang scenario, Kabbalah teaches that every bit of the physical world is comprised of remnants of the single primordial object. Other remarkable similarities between Kabbalah and contemporary science are beyond the scope of this book. But I can tell you that I'm continuously amazed by the extent to which today's cosmologists are arriving at conclusions that Kabbalists taught thousands of years ago!

Rabbi Brandwein saw the Light in everyone. How someone looked or acted on the outside was completely unimportant to him. "Do not look at the container, but search for what is inside. Everyone is worth our time and love." To spread the word of the Creator, it is not necessary to correct others on their spiritual flaws. You simply need to find the deepest point within them and then bestow love. Spirituality will be the natural result.

On another occasion, Rabbi Brandwein and I

went to a factory of the Histadrut, in Yokne'am, where approximately 21,000 people made their living. By this time, I'd given up wondering why we would go to this place or that, and just rode along in the car, excited to see what would happen and what I might learn. Yet I think that a part of me was still categorizing people, and had not yet taken to heart all of my teacher's lessons.

Yokne'am, where we were living at the time, is about 50 miles from Tel Aviv and took about two hours by car. Again, Rabbi Brandwein and the Histadrut factory manager embraced each other immediately. My teacher had already told me that this factory was non-religious, and of course the kitchen was not kosher. Again a small voice within me wondered why we had come, for surely we would not change any minds.

Soon the factory manager began showing us around. It was nearing lunch time, and as we entered the dining area my teacher noticed that a small group of workers was seated apart from the others. This seemed to concern him, and he asked the manager why these people were segregated. It was simple, the manager explained. These people ate only kosher food and so out of respect to them and to prevent their food from being contaminated, he had made a special place for them.

Rabbi Brandwein nodded. He understood this as a logical solution, but he also saw an opening for something he had wanted to say to the factory manager for a long time.

"It is obvious you care deeply for your workers and have great respect for them," he said. "But unfortunately the solution to your problem has created an even greater problem. Now, although your workers who observe kashrut can safely eat their food, they are effectively isolated from everyone else in the factory. The religious and non-religious do not eat together, and because of this they are not likely to form relationships or share with each other. In trying to solve a problem, you have driven people apart and this can only be bad for worker morale in the whole factory."

The factory manager was of course concerned and wanted to know immediately what he should do. Since he and my teacher were old friends and loved each other so deeply, the manager naturally trusted whatever he might suggest and was more than willing to carry it out.

I realize now that my teacher had been counting on this trust and had been waiting for just such a moment as this. "If your entire kitchen were kosher," he said, "all the workers could sit together and eat. Is this not the aim of the Histadrut, to bring workers closer together? I would be happy and honored to contribute money from my own funds to help pay for the koshering of the kitchen."

The factory manager immediately and enthusiastically accepted my teacher's idea. In a very short time, 21,000 workers were eating kosher meals!

If Rabbi Brandwein had simply accepted the situation at the factory as it was, he would never have made the suggestions he did. Instead, he focused on the love and trust that he saw in his friend. As Kabbalah teaches, every person is a vessel, and our task is to see the point of Light within.

"I WAS DRAWN TO KABBALAH AS IF BY A MAGNET...."

From the beginning, I was drawn to the great Kabbalistic texts as if by a magnet. I felt as though I'd found the inner meaning that I'd been searching for my entire life.

This was exactly the sensation I had as Rabbi Brandwein and I began studying Rabbi Yehuda Ashlag's introduction to the *Ten Luminous Emanations*, the first work which he gave me to read. Every night, we discussed the passages that I had read and analyzed the previous morning. Rabbi

Brandwein would wait patiently as I unraveled the book's mysteries, never interrupting or never criticizing, but always gently urging me to see the hidden truth.

Rabbi Ashlag, who had been Rabbi Brandwein's teacher, was also the author of the *Sulam*, one of the great Kabbalistic texts of the 20th century. So, through Rabbi Brandwein, it is accurate to say that I was blessed to receive Rabbi Ashlag's teachings as well, in the same way that the lessons of Kabbalah have passed from teacher to student over the centuries.

It was in the study of this great text that I first learned the Kabbalistic truth that God is Light, and that it is the nature of human beings to *Desire to Receive* this Light for themselves alone. We are Vessels whose very essence is this *Desire to Receive*. If we receive the Light without meriting it, we feel pain and shame. By transforming our *Desire to Receive* for ourselves alone into a *Desire to Receive* for the *Purpose of Sharing*, we extinguish our pain, and ultimately become one with the Creator.

Through study of the *Ten Luminous Emanations,* I became acquainted with these ideas. I can hardly convey how profoundly they moved me. To quote Rabbi Ashlag, "One who studies the Talmud without grasping the secrets of the Torah and its mysteries is like one who sits in the dark without the Light of The Creator shining within him. Only through the wisdom of Kabbalah can one grasp the ultimate purpose of Creation."

But if this were so, why had I never learned these ideas before? Had I not spent my childhood in religious schools and devoted years to the careful study of the Talmud? Late at night in Rabbi Brandwein's study, or walking home through the streets of Jerusalem, I pondered this thought. It was perhaps here that the first seeds of today's Kabbalah Centre were sown, for surely people everywhere deserved to know these important truths.

Yet the wisdom of Kabbalah has traditionally been kept from children in their religious education, since teachers have considered the revealed truth of the Talmud to be far more important than the concealed truth of the *Zohar* and other kabbalistic texts. For this reason, I knew nothing of Kabbalah when Rabbi Brandwein and I began our studies in the early 60s. Yet in those first evenings in Rabbi Brandwein's study, I was struck by the wisdom and truth of Rabbi Ashlag's writings, and felt from the beginning that I had at last found my true nature and calling.

Unfortunately, a short time later, I was forced to return to the United States on a brief business trip, as I was required to do throughout my stay in Israel. I can still recall the emptiness I felt at being separated from Rabbi Brandwein and the great wisdom to which he had introduced me. Forced to remain in the United States for a period of time, I took to calling him on the telephone every day and when I was finally able to return, I felt a necessity to stay constantly by his side.

At first, I was puzzled by these feelings, for I had always been independent by nature. Yet now I would have instantly sacrificed my own life to protect Rabbi Brandwein. The power of the Kabbalah, which came to me through him, was impossible to deny. Through my teacher, I felt the Light of the Holy One, blessed be He, far more than ever before.

What a gifted teacher and advisor Rabbi Brandwein was—never dictating or lecturing to his students, never judging or criticizing them, always giving them space in which to grow, and yet somehow urging them toward levels of wisdom that would otherwise have been unattainable. Because of this quality, people from all walks of life were drawn to him. Even Levi Eshkol, the prime minister at that time, frequently asked Rabbi Brandwein for counsel.

Today, when I'm asked how the Kabbalah Centre has achieved such success in such a short time, I don't have to think very hard for an answer. "Give people breathing space," I say, remembering those first wonderful evenings in my teacher's study. "Listen to them and honor what they have to say. Respect everyone without focusing on or being influenced by their outer appearance. Above all, make enough room in your heart to love each and every person without thinking about what you will get in return."

"WHY EVIL IS DRAWN TO LIGHT"

One day, Rabbi Brandwein took some time out from our busy schedule because he said he had something important to tell me. We were sitting in the courtyard of the synagogue just as the sun was setting. It is difficult to describe the beauty of that moment, the colors of the sunset and the natural beauty that surrounded us. I was also feeling very happy because I knew I had found my teacher and through him, my purpose in life.

"Your mission as my student is a very serious one, which is why I want to talk to you today. I can sense that the Light of Kabbalah shines very brightly in you, and so it is necessary for you to grasp all of my ideas."

"You must remember that it is the purpose of every truly spiritual person to bring the Light of the Blessed One to the world. This is the only way that darkness and negativity can be destroyed. Nothing else works. Expensive weapons, large armies, carefully planned wars—they're all useless, and worse than useless. You must work very hard to fill yourself with Light, because only Light can wipe out the negativity of the world."

As he was speaking, I realized that there are certain moments in which we achieve much greater intimacy with the Light than is usual in our daily lives. As we learn more about Kabbalah and make it a part of everything we do, we learn to recognize these moments and pay them special heed. Although I had just begun my studies, I knew in my heart that this was such a moment.

Rabbi Brandwein continued, "When people hate each other they put out the Light. Unfortunately, throughout history the greatest violence has been among religious groups—the very people who were called upon to protect the Light. Millions of lives have been lost in the name of religion. The forces of darkness and negativity, which some people call the Satan, are drawn to places where the Light gathers, just as flies are drawn to honey. You could almost say that the Satan feeds on

Light, and wherever he is, the place becomes dark very quickly. By destroying Light, the Satan nourishes himself and insures himself a long, healthy existence. Do you understand?"

"I think so."

Rabbi Brandwein stood up and smiled. He had such a warm, gentle smile.

We began walking up the road toward his house as I thought carefully about what he had said. It was now evening. The streetlights came on and in many of the houses you could see families gathered around their tables, eating and talking peacefully.

"So are you saying that places of worship are the most susceptible to this darkness?" I asked him.

"Ironically, yes, since wherever people worship The Creator, sparks of Light are created. Light creates unity, which the Satan wants to fight against, so as soon as an argument breaks out, no matter how small, he is right there to get his meal."

As we continued up the road toward his house I began to understand a portion of Vayishlach that had always puzzled me and now my teacher's words had made clear. The Torah tells us that Jacob and Esau were twins. They were as different as night and day, looking and acting differently in every way.

Jacob led a blessed, righteous life, and was respected in his community, while Esau killed people and committed many other terrible acts.

Vayishlach says that it was a well-known tradition that Esau hated Jacob, but there also came a time when his compassion was stirred and he kissed him with his whole heart. This was very remarkable for Esau, who hated and envied his brother. What puzzled me was this: Was it Esau's choice to hate Jacob? Was he observing some kind of tradition to hate? Hatred has terrible consequences, for example, the First Temple was destroyed by hatred. How could hatred come into being, either through choice or tradition? Once it had come into being, how could it suddenly be transformed, as when Esau kissed his brother with his whole heart?

I understood the meaning behind these questions because of Rabbi Brandwein's lesson. Clearly Esau represented darkness in the story, while Jacob represented Light. And since darkness is drawn to Light—this is a very important spiritual law—that is why Vayishlach refers to Esau's hatred for his brother as a tradition. At the same time he can't help kissing him, because the sparks of Light which Jacob projects are too tempting.

Clearly it is the responsibility of all students of

Kabbalah to project Light. Yet the more Light we project, the more we run the risk of attracting the Satan. This is why my teacher stressed the importance of love and peace. Wherever and whenever conflict arises, he would say, the Satan will be there.

This was only one of many important conversations that I had with Rabbi Brandwein and it gave me much food for thought. He was an even better listener than he was a speaker and was the most talented teacher I have ever experienced. Later, when we entered his home, there was a wholesome, modest meal waiting for us. The table was illuminated by glowing candles and good conversation, and I felt truly blessed.

THE BOW AND ARROW
OF LAG B'OMER

The spring of the Six-Day War was a difficult time for Israel, but also a time of enormous energy. On June 5th,1967 the war broke against Egypt on one front and Jordan and Syria another. The entire war lasted 132 hours and 30 minutes, one of the shortest wars in history. By the end of the war, Israel had acquired Sinai, the Gaza Strip, East Jerusalem, the West Bank, and the Golan Heights.

As the war approached, tensions in the city of

Tel Aviv began to rise and there was fear that the country would be entering a prolonged conflict. Yet inside the Kabbalah Centre, the atmosphere was peaceful. Rabbi Brandwein was deeply involved in his work and I was immersed in my studies. Nonetheless, a few days before the outbreak of the war, the Rabbi decided that we needed to spend Shabbat in Tiberias, and then travel to Meron, in eastern Gallilee, when Shabbat ended. Tiberias was a drive of several hours from Tel Aviv, and Meron would be a few hours more.

I was unclear why my teacher had made this decision, but Rabbi Brandwein explained that the day after Shabbat was the anniversary of the death of Rabbi Shimon bar Yochai, the author of the *Zohar*. To honor the heavenly Rabbi Shimon, we needed to pray in Tiberias and then go on to Meron, where he was buried, for the traditional celebration. Of course, I asked my teacher how we could possibly proceed at night when, by military ordinance, we would not be allowed to even use our headlights. Furthermore, it was clearly dangerous, perhaps even life-threatening for us to be on the road at this time. I knew my protests would have no effect. Whenever Rabbi Brandwein made a decision, he always carried it out.

The drive to Tiberias proved uneventful. Once we left the frantic preparations in Tel Aviv behind us, the trip itself was actually rather relaxed. To pass the time, Rabbi Brandwein began to discuss the story of Rabbi Shimon, and why we honor him each year on the anniversary of his death.

"Did you know," Rabbi Brandwein began, "that Rabbi Shimon was a great teacher of the Torah? We remember him as the author of the *Zohar*, but in fact, he was known throughout Israel for his studies in the revealed wisdom of the Torah as well as the concealed wisdom of Kabbalah. He was the very first to make visible the hidden secrets of the Creator and for this reason the anniversary of his death is a joyful celebration. Children light bonfires and play with bows and arrows, which are the symbols of the holiday—it's truly wonderful!"

Even with the growing tensions, our Shabbat in Tiberius was surprisingly peaceful. The city is on the western edge of the Sea of Galilee. As we calmly strolled on the shore, we had a breathtaking view of the sea, the shoreline, and surrounding mountains. There was a feeling of profound spiritual presence, perhaps because both the Talmud and Mishnah were compiled in Tiberius.

Only a few hours after we arrived, however, the war broke out. Somehow my teacher managed to convince a taxi driver to take us to Meron and we set out as soon as it was dark. The Creator was with us though. There was a hard, bright moon in the sky and we arrived in Meron in under two hours—our first miracle of the night, though there would be many to follow.

The war started and bombs and missiles began to fall, which we had no knowledge of at the time, of course. During that night we simply studied together at various places, and Rabbi Brandwein in particular seemed deep in meditation and prayer. The city of Meron was remarkably quiet, the usual festivities cancelled because of the war, and all around us was great tranquillity and peace.

"This is how every war should be waged," Rabbi Brandwein commented at one point. "With the help of Rabbi Shimon and Rabbi Ashlag, great wonders will be achieved tonight." Only now, years later, do I even have an inkling of what he was attempting—the miracles he was hoping to accomplish with his thoughts.

The next day, we returned to Tel Aviv and because it was a time of emergency, the Rabbi did what he could to help in the community. He stressed throughout, however, that it was only through the study of Kabbalah that we would be able to control the events around us. It was in the places of prayer and meditation, and not on the battlefield, that the real war would be won.

By June 11th, peace had returned. One of the shortest wars in history was over. For years, I have thought about these events, and the meaning of my teacher's words during that time. What had he been implying when he spoke about controlling the events around us, or about winning the war?

A few weeks after the end of the war, Rabbi Brandwein gave me a passage he had written about the celebration of Lag B'Omer, the anniversary of Rabbi Shimon's death, and the significance of the bow and arrow as its symbol.

"Here," he said, handing me his article. "Perhaps this will make clear the events of the past few weeks, and why we had to go to Meron."

I chose a comfortable chair in the Rabbi's study and settled down to read. I knew that what he had given me would explain many things, but after the first page, I admit I was a little disappointed. The article began with a simple explanation of the weapons of war. How could this have any relevance?

I continued reading: "...a person's enemy or prey is not always an arm's length away, and modern weapons deal with this—missiles, rocket launchers and so forth. But the first weapon to hit a distant target was the bow and arrow."

Well, yes. The bow and arrow were the symbols of Lag B'Omer, so perhaps now the article would explain something.

Rabbi Brandwein's article continued: *"This ancient weapon is based on the paradox that the deadly arrow must first be pulled back toward one's own heart in order to strike the heart of the enemy and the more it is drawn toward oneself, the more distant a foe it can reach. To gather strength, the weapon must first be drawn inward. The 'revealed' aspect of Torah is like a close-range weapon that aids us in meeting the obvious challenges of life. But not everything in life is obvious. What of the hidden mysteries, the divine essence of reality? Here we must delve into ourselves, pull inward toward our heart, as the arrow is pulled inward, to the very core of the soul... "*

This is the reason that the bow and arrow are the symbols of Lag B'Omer. The greatest wars are won inside of us, and this is the only place our enemies can ever be truly defeated, even when the odds seem overwhelming. As the *Zohar* states, "So many miracles are performed for us every day of which we're not even aware. It is impossible for the world to exist without miracles".

Regarding this passage, we must remind ourselves of the Kabbalistic definition of a miracle, as distinct from the way the word has come to be used in everyday conversation. Afer all, we've gotten used to hearing that "miracles are everywhere." Television is a miracle, brain surgery is a miracle, computers are a miracle. Kabbalah, however, focuses on intention as a defining characteristic of miracles—and it uses the concept of magic to sharpen this definition. The difference between magic and miracles lies less in what happens than in why it happens. Egypt had magicians who could match the wonders performed by Moses and Aaron, but the acts of the Egyptians were most definitely not miracles, because they were done for self-aggrandizement or out of ego based needs. As a person grows more spiritually powerful and adept in Kabbalistic principles, there is the danger of turning into the kind of ego-attached magician that the Egyptians represented. The true miracle worker, however, does nothing that is not in service of the Lord. In Kabbalah, it is our consciousness that defines and determines the nature of a miracle. In this sense, a single act of kindness performed in resistance to an evil inclination is a far greater miracle than the most powerful computer that will ever be built.

David's seemingly miraculous encounter with the giant Goliath, for example, is really a battle with the ego-Goliath in David himself. His physical victory over the external Goliath is simply an expression of the inner conquest that has already taken place—and that inner conquest is the real miracle. Moreover, this is the same miracle that each of us must bring about in order to fulfill our life's purpose. It is not easy. Nor did the Creator intend for it to be easy.

"THE PERSON WITH NO ENEMIES HAS DONE NOTHING"

Rabbi Brandwein well understood the dangers of speaking your own mind, of standing out from the crowd to do what you believe in, even at the risk of personal danger. "One who has not undergone the pains of spreading the knowledge of Kabbalah has done nothing," he would say. "When the man with no enemies departs this world for the next, The Creator will know immediately that he has wasted his life."

It took me a while to understand what my teacher meant by this. Was it actually necessary to create enemies? Wasn't it better to be well-liked by all, particularly if one hoped to gain spiritual followers and spread the word of The Creator? This was a question that puzzled me for some time until I heard a story about Rabbi Brandwein that revealed his lack of fear in the face of anger and even hatred. In my early life, I had known many deeply frightened people and it was good to finally come face-to-face with such a courageous individual.

Fear is always an instrument of the Satan, according to Kabbalistic teaching. For many religious people, the experience of fear often impels them to call upon the Creator for deliverance. Kabbalah, however, tells us that deliverance from fear resides within our own hearts and not in the heavens. More specifically, Kabbalists use the term *certainty* to denote the spiritual condition that erases fear. The most often-cited Biblical instance of certainty occurs in the Book of Exodus, when the fleeing Hebrews have been driven to brink of the Red Sea by the pursuing Egyptian army. They prayed to G-d to save them and G-d's reply was, "*Why do you cry out to me?*" In other words, the tools of salvation are already in your posession. You must trust them and use them *with absolute certainty*. For the Hebrews, this meant walking into the waters of the sea even up to their very necks, certain in the knowledge that the Creator would deliver them if it was best for their souls. If they were not delivered, it would mean that their true best interests lay elsewhere. In any event, fear denied the power and benevolence of the Creator. For a Kabbalist, fear is not to be trusted and certainly not to be acted upon.

I heard about Rabbi Brandwein's bravery from an old friend of his, who we happened to meet in a most unlikely fashion. Our adventure began very late one night. It was at least one or two o'clock in the morning, and my teacher and I were still busy studying. Rabbi Brandwein would often study until four or five in the morning, when he felt the strength to do so. "It is the sole purpose of each of us to receive the Light of the Kabbalah," he would say. "And then to share it with the world. It is our responsibility. This is the only way that all the darkness and negativity in the world can be destroyed." The lights were glowing brightly inside his small study, but outside the night was very dark and cold.

Suddenly, in the peace and tranquility of his study, he stood up and said that we were going to Jerusalem, to the area of Bethlehem, in order to visit Rachel's tomb. Though he was a very gentle man, but there was a firmness to his voice that was undeniable.

"Right now?" I asked.

He nodded.

I mentioned that the tomb was closed for renovations, but he said that made no difference. This was only a month or two after the end of the Six-

Day War, so of course there was also some tension in the air, though it would be less eventful then our trip to Tiberius.

The drive to Bethlehem was very dark and the streets were almost deserted. When we arrived a few hours later, the gates to Rachel's tomb were closed, as I had predicted, but Rabbi Brandwein sat down on a small bench and waited peacefully. It was almost sunup by now and the sky was growing brighter.

Before long a guard appeared and asked if he could open the gate for us. This was something else about Rabbi Brandwein that always surprised me, how confident he was that his purposes would be realized. Inside the tomb he stood quietly and with great reverence for quite some time. Then we headed into the city, where he said he had an important errand to accomplish.

Instead of going into the Israeli section of the city, however, we headed into the Arab quarter. Where was he taking us? Surely my teacher wasn't also friends with Arabs? Here again my conservative background was rearing its head. Unity between different sects of a single religion was a worthy goal, but how could there be unity between different religions? I thought I had cleansed myself of divisive instincts during our visit to the Histadrut factory, but I was wrong.

As it happened, Rabbi Brandwein took me to visit an old friend of his named Jurbin, who lived in a large apartment in the center of the Arab quarter. Glowing with happiness at the Rabbi's visit, Jurbin told him he had waited twenty years to meet him again, and to honor him he gave him a large box of beautiful grapefruit from his father's grove outside the city. They hugged and kissed each other with tremendous warmth, expressing a love between people of different cultures and religions that was wonderful to see.

Rabbi Brandwein was greatly loved by all of Jurbin's family and then spent some time visiting with his friend's children, while Jurbin sat with me and told me the story of the Rabbi's great courage. In 1936, the economic situation in Israel had been very bad, as it was around the world. My teacher had taken a job in construction, something unheard of for a great scholar, but it was a job he loved. Often he smiled and said, "When I am high on the scaffolding of buildings, I feel a spiritual elevation too. It is the time I can truly come to know and love my fellow human beings."

Unfortunately, not everyone in Israel had the

opportunity for such jobs. Some people did not even have enough money to buy bread, and this had been Jurbin's situation. He had a young family to feed and literally no way to make money. Then one day he heard about the "Construction Rabbi." Even among Arabs, Rabbi Brandwein was known as a man who did not hold prejudices against his brothers.

Of course, there were no Arab workers on the construction site, and some of the workers had very vehement political views. In addition, the laws of the Histadrut union at that time stipulated that only non-Arabs could be employed. Nonetheless, Rabbi Brandwein was eager to help Jurbin obtain work in construction, despite the dangers this action could cause. At worst, he could lose his own job, and if it were found out, he would certainly inspire the hatred of the other workers and create enemies.

For a cover-up, he gave Jurbin the Hebrew name of Isaac, since that was something an Arab would never call himself. Thus, Jurbin began a long relationship with the construction union, which fed his family throughout the depression. The only problem came when the workers would need a minyan, which is the spiritual quorum of ten Jewish men necessary for a religious service. Then he would conveniently disappear!

On the way back to Tel Aviv the next day, Rabbi Brandwein told me about his own teacher Rabbi Ashlag, and how he had also confronted risk in order to follow the teachings of the Kabbalah. Once he had even been beaten up inside a place of worship and greatly persecuted, simply for espousing his beliefs. When Rabbi Brandwein began studying with his master at the age of 20, he needed to go from the Old City of Jerusalem, where he was living at the time, to Givat Shaul, where Rabbi Ashlag lived. Of course there were convenient bus lines which connected these two sections, but his teacher was so disliked, that drivers in the bus union were pressured by Rabbi Ashlag's enemies to change the route. As a result, Rabbi Brandwein was forced to walk for two hours, every time he wanted to study Kabbalah. It was a price he was happy to pay, however, for the chance to be near his teacher.

All those who spread the word of Kabbalah and speak their minds are made to suffer, and The Creator be praised that I too have experienced the pain of hatred. We must all remember, however, that if one has not undergone the pain of spreading the knowledge of Kabbalah, one has done nothing. In the days of the Messiah, darkness and negativity will certainly rise up to destroy one who does, and our single line of defense will be the wisdom and Light of the Kabbalah.

Only Kabbalah can bring the Messiah, and only Kabbalah can bring peace. This is why darkness so relishes the destruction of Light, since in extinguishing Light he ensures his own survival. When we speak of the Kabbalah, we will naturally bring forth those who oppose us. In fact, it is a sign that we are doing our work correctly. It is an opportunity, not a deprivation. But we who study and teach Kabbalah should never look for gratitude. On the contrary, we must be aware that our work may bring us hatred, disgrace, and even persecution. But this should cause us joy, not alarm, for only then will we know we have been successful.

"THE UNITY OF THE SOUL"

"The concealed aspect of the Torah, which is Kabbalah, has the power to penetrate to the heart of every human being and to touch their souls," Rabbi Brandwein told me one day. "We exist on this earth as physical bodies, but within us are our souls, and our souls are a part of the Creator. Since there is only one Creator, and because we are all connected to him in this way, we are therefore connected to each other. All of us, all of our souls—no matter how divided we may appear to be—exist in unity. The potential to express this unity, to experience it every moment of our lives, lies within every soul. Just as the souls of Adam and Eve contained all the souls to come in a single unity, so each of us contains the unity of The Creator."

I had now been studying with Rabbi Brandwein for some time. I thought I had grasped these extraordinary concepts, but I did not realize their full meaning until a celebration of Chanukah, which we attended together shortly after the Six-Day War.

So many thoughts which were racing through my mind as we went to this celebration. Since the age of 13, for example, I had wondered about the appearance of the Messiah. When all around me was destruction and dissension, religion fighting religion, and even members of the same religion desperately fighting each other, why would the Messiah choose to appear? In addition I had read in the *Zohar* that when the Messiah appears, war will continue, and the Messiah himself will be a target. So how could he agree to return?

These were some of the questions in my mind as we entered the holiday season. But I was also full of excitement and anticipation. Rabbi Brandwein had decided it was time for us to leave Tel Aviv and return to the Old City in Jerusalem, which Israel had acquired during the war. Using his contacts in the Workers' Union, he found a run-down building which the workers offered to repair. Little did I know that Rabbi Brandwein would only live in this building for a few months, before he was to pass away—peacefully and with the grace of The Creator. But that is another story. When we entered the Old City, we were the first settlers to return.

Though repairs on the building were still not complete, we took up residence and began preparation for our holiday celebrations. Rabbi Brandwein did not view holidays as a time to commemorate past events: Instead, they were unique and powerful occasions for connecting with the Light, and when we in our prayers can feel the Creator's presence most strongly. I can still remember our small place of worship inside the building. Not all of our furniture had arrived, but the light from our candles fell on the floor in a mix of delicate colors, echoing the Light of The Creator as we prayed. All of us were greatly uplifted by Rabbi Brandwein's words that evening, and inside the silence of our new building, devoid of furniture but not of love. I had the sensation that something new for the world was surely taking shape.

A few days later, the Rabbi and all of his students were invited to a holiday celebration by the

Workers' Union, to be held in the Habima Hall in Tel Aviv. The Union, of course, was not a religious group, and I was curious to see how successful my teacher would be with people who observed not one of the religious holidays during the year. When we arrived at the Hall, however, all the workers rose to a standing ovation that lasted several minutes, and the reception by the union leadership was equally impressive. An astonishing thought crossed my mind: "They are treating him like the long awaited Messiah!"

As Rabbi Brandwein began to speak, the hundreds of workers fell silent. It was the holiday of the lighting of the candles, and a candelabra stood in front of him, with its flames flickering softly across his face.

"As I speak to you, gaze at these flames," he said. "Tiny, silent, glowing. Sometimes dancing, vulnerable, yet always reaching upwards. Each of you is like a flame, because you possess an energy that continually reaches upward, and that is your soul. Let yourself feel your own flame—a flame that wants to touch something that is higher and richer and deeper. That is the flame of your true self and it can never be extinguished. On this day of Chanukah, we do not simply commemorate a past victory in a conflict. Instead, we take the opportunity to feel the Light of The Creator which burns more brightly than ever."

The hall was silent, everyone united in rapt attention. At that moment, I began to fully understand the concept of Unity, and the reason why the Messiah will surely appear, even amid fighting and dissension. It is because the concealed world of our souls has the potential to exist in unity, and this unity is literally a part of The Creator.

When Rabbi Brandwein accepted his position as the spiritual head of the Workers' Union, there had been such great criticism and dissension among other religious leaders. Why was he legitimizing a secular group by agreeing to become its rabbi? Hadn't the union desecrated religious holidays and spread the practice of eating non-kosher food through the popular restaurants they owned? The longer he remained their spiritual leader, the louder the criticism and anger grew, until his enemies were everywhere.

However, my teacher's resolve was firm. He knew that within each of the Union members, a soul existed that could be united with other souls. When the suggestion was first made that he accept the position of spiritual leader, the offer had come as a complete surprise. He told me, "And at the same time I realized that I had prayed for this for 30 years—that all of Israel would return to religion—and so I agreed. For as it is said by the sages, *'The many can only be redeemed by becoming one'*."

"KABBALAH IS FOR ALL PEOPLE, NOT JUST A CHOSEN FEW"

One night, during a break during our studies, I took the opportunity to ask Rabbi Brandwein a very basic question: "Why are you concerned with the non-religious? Isn't it their business whether or not they choose to study and learn the ways of the Creator? As you yourself have commented on numerous occasions, we are not the spiritual policemen of the universe."

He cleared his voice and sat comfortably in a chair. I knew by his actions that he was preparing himself for a long explanation, and indeed, my simple question gave way to a long discussion that lasted well into the night. Throughout his discourse, I listened carefully, and when I returned to my room I wrote down everything I could remember, as precisely as possible. What follows, then, is his answer to me, to the best of my recollection:

He began by discussing the war and destruction of the 20th century which in his opinion had caused the worst suffering and devastation of all time. From the development and use of nuclear weapons, to the Holocaust, to the bloody world wars and the many ethnic genocides, this was truly a century of pain, unparalleled in history in its darkness. While our masters of the past rested peacefully in the belief that the wisdom of Kabbalah would be revealed to us in the end of days, this was no longer a belief we could comfortably share. Misfortune overwhelmed us from both within and without.

"To make matters worse, the younger generation is slipping away from us," he explained. Rabbi Brandwein was truly a pure-hearted Kabbalist. I later discovered that many of the ideas he shared that night were already written in his introduction to *The Writings of the Ari*, the great 16th century Kabbalist Rabbi Isaac Luria, who was known as "The Ari", which means the lion.

"There has never been a time when all at once a suppressed hatred was released upon one single group of people, wherever they could be found," Rabbi Brandwein continued, referring of course to the Holocaust. "This terrible event requires us to search our souls in order to cause 'an awakening from below.' We must make an effort to spread our knowledge amongst all peoples, so that every nation will worship The Creator and obey His laws and precepts. Only in this way can we hope to banish the darkness."

For this reason, he explained, he had done something that no one else had ever attempted: He had brought the study of Kabbalah to the common man. He had taken it out of the ivory tower where it had been locked away for over 2,000 years, and brought it into the world.

This revolutionary step was absolutely necessary, he explained, since the all the misfortunes of the world—poverty, destruction, murder—could literally be erased by the wisdom of the Kabbalah. Thousands of passages in the *Zohar* made this clear.

"The delay of our redemption and all the evil that besets us is due to the neglect of the current generation to their lack of interest in holy study," Rabbi Brandwein continued. With the help of The Creator, it was up to us to change that. And this was the reason that he had accepted the spiritual leadership of the Workers' Union, as part of his sacred mission to spread the wisdom of Kabbalah. Kabbalah was for all people, not just a chosen few. Moreover, we were blessed in our generation to have access to the writings of Rabbi Brandwein's own teacher and mentor, Rabbi Yehuda Halevy Ashlag, whose writings explain Kabbalah in simple direct language that all can understand.

Despite constant objections from all sides, Rabbi Brandwein understood that it was time to act. "It is written, *'They have made void your Torah'*," he said, "and therefore all the children of The Creator must begin to study Kabbalah.

'They have made void your Torah'—how can we interpret this passage? It is an overwhelmingly tragic but undeniable fact that the last hundred years have brought calamities such as never before in human history. For the Jewish people, the Holocaust is the most pertinent example, but we must never forget that millions of non-Jews perished in the Holocaust as well. Moreover, dictators such as Stalin and Mao killed even more people than Hitler, though numbers are irrelevant, since murdering even one person is like destroying an entire universe. Perhaps Rabbi Brandwein saw that the tradition of Torah study that had predominated into the 20th century—that is, the study of the revealed Torah— had been brought to an end by the catastrophes and atrocities of our time. Perhaps he saw that a new and more powerful weapon of the Light must now be brought into the battle against Darkness, and this weapon is of course Kabbalah.

I also believe there was another reason for his

deep belief that Kabbalah must be brought to the world at large, and this was his genuine and instinctive love of people. Only his love of others could have convinced the Workers' Union not to celebrate their annual ball on the eve of the most important spiritual holiday of the year, or encouraged them to serve Kosher meals in their restaurants. Like the Gaon sage and teacher Rabbi Yaakov Tzemach, who was another of his great inspirations, Rabbi Brandwein understood that, "...the purpose of the wisdom [of Kabbalah] is to provide us with protection in these dangerous times, and to lead us to a newfound closeness with our Father in Heaven."

Kabbalah teaches that, in generations gone by, people were more spiritual by nature. Their intuitive piety saved them from the levels of persecution that have taken place in modern times. Now that we have drifted far from our spiritual foundations, our protection must come from study and practical use of this wonderful and profound wisdom. And wisdom, Kabbalah tells us, is available to us throughout creation, but we must gain awareness of its presence through humility and sincere desire to learn. In the *Zohar* there are several passages in which great teachers appear in unexpected forms: a child, for example, or a menial worker, or even a donkey—but their lessons should by no means be ignored! "The wise man is he who learns from all men," according to the Talmud, and Kabbalah teaches us that wisdom is the power to see "the end in the beginning." The Creator has already seen everything that will ever happen. But we also have the free will to prevent it from happening that way. This is a paradox that takes us to the heart of Kabbalistic wisdom.

May The Creator protect us and forgive our sins.

"THE DIRECTION AND AIM OF PRAYER"

On the night of March 20, 1969, peacefully and with the grace of The Creator, Rabbi Brandwein moved on from this world to the next. There was no warning; his loving heart simply gave out. He returned his pure soul to his Creator between the walls of his new school in Jerusalem, the city to which he had come so many years before to study with his own teacher Rabbi Ashlag. I had spent only a few years with him, yet in that time, he had given me everything. His last gift proved to be the most long-lasting: the focus and direction for my prayer.

Shortly before his death, he had moved his study center from Tel Aviv to the Old City of Jerusalem, which puzzled me at the time. What could be his purpose in doing this? At the close of the Six-Day War, he had arranged through his connections in the Workers' Union, to purchase a building for his school as well as his living quarters. Why would he want to locate himself in an area of a different religion and people? It made no sense to me.

He was there for less than a year before he died because of the time required for the renovations on the building. Immediately after his death, the Rabbi who replaced him at the Workers' Union bought the building. This man rarely visited or used the building, and it was soon sold by the Workers' Union. Over the years, it was bought and sold again and again. To this very day, it remains empty and unused. It has stood now in the Old City of Jerusalem for over 30 years, barely different from how it looked when Rabbi Brandwein first moved in. Its high ceilings and gracious windows look out on a patio below. Inside the room we once used for our synagogue, I envision only silence and peace.

For many years, I remained mystified as to why these events unfolded as they did. Was there another, deeper purpose behind Rabbi Brandwein's purchase of the building? Why has it gone unused as long as it has?

To answer this question, I need to tell a story

which happened a month or so before Rabbi Brandwein's death. One evening during our studies, Rabbi Brandwein gave me several texts concerning the importance of the nation of Israel to our prayers and to the following of all of The Creator's commandments. At the time this was outside our scope of study, but the material seemed important to Rabbi Brandwein, and I accepted it without question.

"Please never forget this," he said, "even after you return to America permanently."

"I will never return to America permanently," I tried to argue. "I will be by your side forever." But he paid no attention.

One of the texts was a Tractate Ketubot, or Talmudic marriage contract, which stated that, "Whoever lives in the land of Israel is as one who has The Creator. And whoever lives outside the land of Israel is like one who does not have The Creator." Rabbi Brandwein pointed out that many texts echoed this same theme: the importance of Israel to living a correct spiritual path. In a portion of the Devarim, for example, the sage Rashi states that even after, "...you have gone into exile, you must excel in the various spiritual precepts, so that those commandments will not be new to you when you return."

These texts, Rabbi Brandwein said, are telling us that the prayer of a person who lives outside of Israel is not proper, and that if one keeps a commandment outside Israel, it is as if he never kept it at all. We follow the commandments correctly in preparation for our return to Israel—so we will be accustomed, for example, to saying a particular prayer or keeping the Sabbath when we return. This is similar to children's first learning spiritual practices. In the beginning they might feel uncomfortable or awkward, but with practice the commandments will become second nature. In the same way we must prepare ourselves, so that we will be spiritually ready for our return.

I felt in his discussion that he was preparing me for something—a separation possibly—that I did not want to even consider. Long ago, I had resolved that I would protect Rabbi Brandwein with my very life, and so the thought of separation was abhorrent to me. At the same time, I wanted to carefully absorb his lesson, since I knew that everything he said to me would be of great worth in the years to come.

"Excuse me, rabbi," I said as tactfully as possible, "but as you know I intend to celebrate Shabbat with you always, here in Israel. Only my trips to the

United States on business will ever interfere with this. And even that is a problem, since in the States I am ready to say the Shabbat prayers just as you are waking in the morning. So the separation from both you and Israel seems to me greater than ever."

My teacher touched my hand.

"I want you to look carefully around this room," he said.

We were sitting in the synagogue of the new building, with its high ceilings and arched windows. In front of us was the simple altar I had quickly grown to love, with its beautiful, timeworm ark and candelabras. I wanted never to leave it.

"This is the room that should be in your mind always as you pray. When you are in America saying your prayers, you will actually be here with me. According to what Kabbalah teaches us, time and space are only perceptions, not realities. In the Upper Worlds, time and space do not exist. Whenever you pray in the future, where ever you are, you must first create the awareness that you are in the synagogue of this building—which I promise will be as it is now, and will never change. Create this picture clearly and absolutely in your mind, and in this way you will truly be with me. Remember, differences in time and space are mere illusions.

Wherever you are, we will be together."

It is amazing that my teacher was actually referring to extremely advanced concepts in cosmology and physics which have only been recently accepted as true: that we live in an "all at once" universe, where our human perception of time is simply an illusion. The great Kabbalist The Ari, Rabbi Isaac Luria knew this 500 years ago, but it has taken the rest of the world of science centuries to arrive at this realization.

Many stories in the *Zohar* take place in what might be called a quantum world of parallel universes, flying supernatural beings, and startling ellipses of time and space. Within the consciousness–created reality of the *Zohar* however, this is entirely consistent. Kabbalah teaches that time and space are functions of spiritual rather than physical laws. Just as consciousness can cause the Red Sea to part, and just as the Light can cancel the presence of darkness, the limits we have come to expect in our lives can be transcended by a higher awareness. It is interesting to note that time literally means nothing to the Patriarchs and Matriarchs of the Bible. Biblical references to time should never be taken literally. The fact that Biblical characters live to very advanced ages, for example, does not refer to the number of years their hearts had been beating. Rather, their age is an expression of their spiritual attainments.

As Rabbi Brandwein worked with his papers a few feet away, I watched in admiration of his ability to express total concentration and complete serenity at the same time. His movements were so quiet and graceful that I did not hear him several moments later, when he gathered his things and left for the night. I was the one who closed the synagogue that night, to return to my apartment in Tel-Aviv where I was living at the time.

For many days after, Rabbi Brandwein's words echoed in my mind. From that day to the present, wherever I have prayed, I have remained first of all inside that building in Old Jerusalem, which has remained silent and welcoming to all who traveled there in their thoughts and prayers. It is now clear to me why, so many years before, he purchased this building—so that those of us who wander in spiritual exile would have a home to which we can always return, if only in our prayers. And this is also the reason why I recently introduced, into every branch of the Kabbalah Centre, photographs of the burial sites of righteous people and of Kabbalists— so that the land of Israel could be brought closer to us in our spirituality.

Thanks to the merit of Rabbi Brandwein,

today thousands upon thousands of us pray in Israel, oblivious to the constraints of time and space, even while our physical selves remain outside the country.

"I SAW THE FACE OF MY TEACHER OF BLESSED MEMORY SHINE LIKE THE RADIANCE OF THE FIRMAMENT"

My teacher often told me that if I truly wanted to know of the rightness of my actions, I must look around at the kind of opposition I was facing. If unrighteous people opposed me, then I could be sure I was really achieving something worthwhile.

The process of publishing Rabbi Yehuda Halevy Ashlag's handwritten manuscripts of the *Ten Luminous Emanations*, or The Study of Ten Sefirot, has provided many examples of this opposition. Today we have the privilege of reading this work due to the problems and suffering that Rabbi Brandwein was forced to endure.

As we know Rabbi Ashlag, Rabbi Brandwein's teacher and the author of *The Sulam*, had also left behind his *Ten Luminous Emanations*, though in manuscript form only. He never had a chance to publish it before his death. Because my own teacher, however, was sure that its publication would benefit the vast numbers of people who had forsaken their spirituality, he became committed to this idea. In fact, he predicted that this book would be a major force in re-igniting spirituality around the world. During the last year of his life, he began to work on the manuscripts and wrote an introduction in preparation for printing all 16 volumes.

The Satan was well aware that a work of greatness was in the making and opposition quickly arose. Initially, one of Rabbi Ashlag's relatives opposed the very idea of Rabbi Brandwein printing the book. But Rabbi Brandwein had been Rabbi Ashlag's most distinguished student, so who else could have carried out the job? As I later discovered, the relatives of Rabbi Ashlag had once asked Rabbi Ashlag to teach them in the same way that he had instructed my teacher, and Rabbi Ashlag had politely refused, suggesting instead that they study with Rabbi Brandwein. They were very offended, and Rabbi Brandwein was now paying the price. It reminded me of a story I once heard about the Ari, Kabbalist Rabbi Isaac Luria. One day, someone came to him and made a similar request—could he study with him—and instead of answering yes, Rabbi Luria said he must learn from a different rabbi. The man never forgave him.

Rabbi Ashlag's relative even sued Rabbi

Brandwein and actually took him to court in Tel Aviv to stop the publication of the *Ten Luminous Emanations*! Throughout the trial, Rabbi Brandwein was not allowed to speak, not even to stand, and when the judge finally gave a verdict against him, he thought, "Judge, now I am obliged to sit. Yet the time will come when you will also be seated."

A few months later, this same judge was caught stealing. An astounding scandal, yet my teacher had foreseen all these developments.

In the end, Rabbi Brandwein came to an agreement with the relative and the *Ten Luminous Emanations* was published. We can only thank The Creator that it did not share the fate of Rabbi Ashlag's many other manuscripts, which to this day remain in storage, many greatly damaged.

The power of our thought and our determination, is a holy tool that can never be broken. For as Kabbalah teaches, the power of thought can surely transcend the illusions of time, space, and motion. I had been very angry when the Workers' Union sold Rabbi Brandwein's building. How could they let this property go when it belonged to my teacher, and especially since their goals were purely monetary? Ever since that time, however, I have been able to pray in that building every day, and it has been over 30 years now. Today, the Kabbalah Centre has expanded to all corners of the globe. I know this success would not have been possible without the constant help of Rabbi Brandwein and Rabbi Ashlag before him. They continue to work in our lives at every moment.

A few weeks before Rabbi Brandwein's passing, I happened to enter his study late one night, and I saw his face shining with the splendor of the firmament.

"What happened?" I asked him in surprised.

He gazed at me so peacefully, and out of his eyes I could see a wonderful light. "I have finished preparing the last volume of the *Ten Luminous Emanations* for printing," he said. "The work is now complete."

That night, our teacher, the great Rabbi Ashlag came to Rabbi Brandwein in a dream. He kissed his forehead lightly, and said a blessing of holiness without words. That same evenng, I also dreamed of Rabbi Ashlag. In my dream the rabbi visited me, and said that Rabbi Brandwein was the incarnation of Rabbi Moshe Chaim Luzzato, a great 18th century Kabbalist. Rabbi Luzzato's great work, *The Path of the Just*, bespoke a dedication to the Creator rarely found in our time. He wrote about Jewish ethics

and spirituality—and a way of life which few modern people see as their goal.

The next morning we both recounted our
dreams and were greatly moved. The first volume of
The *Ten Luminous Emanations* was published on
1969.

THERE WILL BE A PERSON TO EXPLAIN HIS BOOKS

Our potential to help and share with others is
at first hidden, and we are first unaware of our true
ability in this regard.   Only through service to the
Creator does that potential become manifest.

In the years we studied together, my teacher
always explained the *Ten Luminous Emanations* to me
in a straightforward manner. He primarily focused
on ideas and themes and did not use many examples
or stories to make his point. However, when I began
to teach, my method was entirely different. I used
many stories and illustrative points, but I never prepared them, and I still don't to this day.   In some
mysterious and wonderful way, the seven years I
spent with Rabbi Brandwein gave me a wonderful
gift for communicating the ideas of Kabbalah, as
though my teacher were actually placing his ideas in
my mind and speaking through my lips.

How did I merit this gift, and why was I given the burden of spreading Kabbalah to so many people? I have thought long and hard about these questions and can only say that during all my time with Rabbi Brandwein, I never thought about my own needs where the needs of my teacher were concerned. And it is because of this faithfulness and devotion to him, that I believe he has never left me. It is true that there was a short period after his death when I lost confidence—and the work of Kabbalah felt strange without his presence, but I quickly regained my voice, and since then he has never left me. I have felt him beside me and his voice within me from that moment since.

"So many people in the world today have lost their faith," Rabbi Brandwein often said. "Rabbi Ashlag's purpose, and my purpose after him, has been to restore that faith, by making Kabbalah comprehensible to the average person. The people of the world cannot carry on without spirituality. I do not understand why in all this time, someone has not brought forth the great and obvious remedy to this problem, Kabbalah, and the great book of Kabbalah, the holy *Zohar*. Instead, the very scholars who have access to this healing medicine either withhold it, or write inaccuracies about it, which make it impossible for the average person to return to spirituality."

Only a miracle could reverse this process, Rabbi Brandwein would say, and it was the miracle of Kabbalah itself. Two thousand years ago, Rabbi Shimon bar Yochai said the redemption of humanity was at hand. Rabbi Ashlag and the other great sages had worked all their lives to make this possible. The centuries of our exile from spirituality would soon be over.

A few days after Rabbi Brandwein and I had finished preparing Rabbi Ashlag's book for publication, Rabbi Brandwein took me into his private study. He said he had something important to say to me and that he wanted me to pay close attention.

He closed his eyes for a moment to focus his thoughts, which he often did when he was concentrating. "Rabbi Ashlag once told me that someone would appear who would explain his books completely and perfectly—so perfectly that everyone would at last be brought back to spirituality. And I have decided that person is you."

Rabbi Brandwein held my gaze steadily. I could not turn away. What he had just told me was hard to believe, and yet his words had been clear and unmistakable.

"Your gift and your duty," he said, "is to explain Kabbalah in such a way that all people will easily understand. You have merited this gift with your devotion and faithfulness. I want you to accept it and use it."

I nodded but remained silent. In reality, I was speechless. It was a great responsibility that he gave me that day but, thanks to The Creator, I have been able to carry it out. Since that afternoon in Rabbi Brandwein's study, more than 30 years have passed. Literally hundreds of thousands of people have been returned to spirituality, and the number grows daily.

Of course, none of this would have been possible without my dear wife, my soulmate and the foundation of my home, Rabbanit Karen, blessed among women, who has been by my side always. Some of the most beautiful teachings in the *Zohar* describe the existence of a perfect match, a soulmate, for every human being. How do soulmates find one another in order to fulfill their special destiny? The sages explain that this may take many lifetimes, and may even include some very difficult marriages! Sometimes the "rightness" of soulmates coming together may not be apparent to the world, or even to the individuals themselves. Each of us has an obligation to search for our soulmate to the best of our ability, for this union has been mandated by the Creator Himself. Kabbalah even describes a special angel whose only responsibility is bringing soulmates together.

According to Rabbi Brandwein, the difference between this generation and all the ones that have come before is that now everyone—not only the privileged or special—will help to bring the Messiah. As it is written in the *Zohar*, "We will find that in the last generations that come, the Torah will be forgotten from among them but all those wise at heart will be gathered away to their right places and none will be found who will know how to open or close the Torah. Woe to that generation. And from here on, there will not be such a generation till the generation when the Messiah comes. Then the knowledge will be awakened in the world, as it is written, 'they shall all know Me, from the least of them to the greatest of them.'"

THE ABUNDANCE OF THE SPRINGS OF LIFE

"Once Jacob forgot a small vessel by the side of a river. When he realized it was missing, he went back to find it because though it was not worth much money, he knew even this small object contained sparks of the Creator's Light. He knew that sparks of holiness are present everywhere, in people, animals, plants, and even rocks and pebbles. He did not wish to treat carelessly any of the Light of the

Creator. No matter how small, each of the sparks must be valued and honored."

This was a story from the Torah that Rabbi Brandwein always told, when he wanted to explain why we all need to work hard to return the world to spirituality. This can never be done with boycotts or demonstrations, or any kind of angry protest, he said. Rather, each person must simply be treated with love and respect.

On one occasion, this point was made very clearly and forcefully. The mayor of Tel Aviv had asked Rabbi Brandwein to sit on the religious council for the city, and the Chief Rabbi of Tel Aviv was discussing the allocation of religious funds. He was concerned because 90 percent of the council's budget was given over to administrative duties, with only ten percent left for religious activities. The Rabbi wanted to know why.

He continued, "Look at the example of Rabbi Brandwein. His budget from the Workers' Union was divided exactly the opposite, with 90 percent for religious requirements and only ten percent for administration? Why couldn't Tel Aviv do better?"

When the mayor asked Rabbi Brandwein to respond, he told the story of Jacob and his vessel. No matter how small, Jacob valued each of the sparks of Light from his vessel, because they were holy and came from the Creator. "This is what some people do not understand," he said. "Everything and everyone must be valued, rather than argued about and fought over."

Not long after this, Rabbi Brandwein and I went to bathe in King David's spring in Ein Gedi, an ancient oasis on the shores of the Dead Sea. Although at first this seemed unrelated to the discussion in the religious council, the two events became joined in my mind to highlighting the importance of these ideas.

The bath in Ein Gedi was an ancient historical site. David and his men had found refuge there from the forces of King Saul. The *mikveh*, or ritual bath, which grows out of the spring has always been considered especially purifying and holy. Today, the area is quite striking and beautiful, though much of the water for the *mikveh* is now redirected as irrigation for local farming.

I should explain and emphasize that the *mikveh* is essential to true spirituality, and to all precepts in the Torah, though it has unfortunately fallen out of fashion in modern times. For, as it is written, "He who sets his heart on becoming purified becomes pure as soon as he has immersed himself in the waters of a *mikveh*. As soon as he consents in his heart to bring his soul into the waters of reason, he is pure."

The day was beautiful in Ein Gedi, with a crystal blue sky, bright sun, and water bubbling out of the ancient spring. A large sign, however, made it quite apparent this water was not for public use.

There were others besides my teacher and myself who stood by the oasis, probably because the day was so lovely: workers and students, young men and fathers. They were all talking happily and enjoying the goodness of The Creator which lay before them, but also looking a bit sadly at the running water which they were barred from using, though for centuries their ancestors had bathed in it. I was staring at the water in the same way.

Suddenly I heard a rustling beside me, and when I turned I saw that my teacher was taking off all of his clothes except his underwear preparing to dip into the *mikveh*.

"Come," he said. "It is time to bathe."

"But the sign...."

Of course he didn't answer, and simply stepped into the refreshing spring water, a soft smile on his face.

There was nothing to do but follow.

As the water touched me a sense of tremendous peace and purification came over me. A moment or two later, I turned and saw that many of the men around us, who up till now had been waiting on the shore, were taking off their clothes and were preparing to enter the water.

What great lessons Rabbi Brandwein taught that day: First, when you decide to do a good thing you must do it, without letting anything stop or distract you. But more important, the blessed and healing waters of the Creator have always been essential to the recovery of our spirituality, and Rabbi Brandwein helped me to see that once again. We must use this divinely-given tool!

A few years later, when the gates of Kabbalah were opened to all who wanted to taste from the Tree of Life, the Rabbinit Karen and I organized spiritual tours for all of our students. As part of our tours, we added the *mikveh* of the holy Ari, also known as the spring of Rabbi Yishmael. It was used by the Ari, the great Rabbi Isaac Luria, more than 500 years ago, and today its water is considered so holy that drops of it are taken to other *mikvaot*. Even a single drop of the water can add greatness.

Rabbi Brandwein knew that dipping in any

water could bring holiness; as Jacob said, every spark contains Light. This was true even for the swimming pool of a hotel!

On our way back from Ein Gedi that day, my teacher told me about a great argument that broke out in Jerusalem once because a hotel was being built and the owners planned a swimming pool. At the time, Rabbi Brandwein said, no other hotel in Jerusalem had a swimming pool and this was a great novelty. There were also no natural bodies of water in Jerusalem, as there were in Tel Aviv, and this also caused great excitement. Finally, there would be a place to swim!

On the other hand, many conservative rabbis organized boycotts and demonstrations, asserting that the swimming pool was a religious offense. This was particularly true if men and women would be swimming together. Rabbi Brandwein, however, disagreed. He knew that the majority of people had already abandoned their spirituality, and that demonstrations would change nothing. In fact, they would only serve to drive the people further away. The only way to draw people is with love, he said. Force of any kind simply does not work.

Rabbi Brandwein was happy about the hotel swimming pool because dipping in it could be considered immersion in a *mikveh*. This is the way of a Kabbalist. His main concern was for the well-being of others. But this was also why he was so hated by others. The jealousy he provoked was widespread and lies were frequent and vicious.

I FOUND MY TEACHER FOR LIFE

During the wonderful years I spent with Rabbi Brandwein, I came to understand an important teaching: "The service of the Torah is greater than its study." What did I ever do to merit this time with my teacher? The answer to this question is beyond me. I only know that I served him with all my heart, body, and soul. I had studied in my religious tradition since the age of three, but had never before been offered wisdom such as his.

The power of love is truly great. Yet the more love Rabbi Brandwein had to give, the more obstacles were put in his way. For example, when Rabbi Brandwein was made Head Rabbi of the Workers' Union, the other Rabbis of Tel Aviv were furious. How could a serious, orthodox Rabbi, schooled in Kabbalah, preside over such a non-religious, secular group? Even today, more than 40 years later, there are Rabbis who remain angry with him for taking the position.

In fact, they were so angry (and foolish) that that a few of them actually arranged to call Rabbi Brandwein every Shabbat afternoon, with the sole purpose of disturbing him. It was time to act, they said to each other. It was necessary to stop Rabbi Brandwein's great sin. What nonsense! Of course, my teacher was not fooled. When he understood what was going on, he simply disconnected the telephone line before Shabbat and reconnected it afterwards. Once Rabbi Brandwein was walking in the neighborhood and a man stopped him and asked why he did not pick up the telephone on Shabbat. Surely he was home. Rabbi Brandwein greeted him kindly but otherwise did not respond.

Another time, an invitation to the circumcision ceremony of his grandson was not given to him until 20 minutes before the ceremony was scheduled to start. This exemplifies the degree of pettiness that surrounded him. The depth of anger and hatred. Just at the last moment, someone called him, thinking I suppose that he would never get there in time. Nor was he angry. He managed to arrive at the beginning of the prayers. The Rabbi was not affected by such negative behavior. He was above all that.

Like most people, I have always believed that we should care for and respect others—especially those close to us, like family and friends. But what about strangers? If we do not know another person, do they deserve the same care and concern as those close to us? Should we love them as well?

I had never seriously considered this idea before I met my teacher. Though the concept is difficult for most people to put into practice, this was the true core of Rabbi Brandwein's teaching.

I had been searching all my life for a master who could direct me to a higher level of spirituality. Finally, I met Rabbi Brandwein and knew immediately that I had found my teacher for life. Since that day, even death has not caused me to leave his side.

THE POWER OF RESTRICTION AND THE BREAD OF SHAME

Rabbi Brandwein told me this story. There was once a great spiritual scholar and teacher by the name of Rabbi Akiva. His students were considered to be the brightest and most gifted spiritual scholars of their day. There were 24,000 of them and they studied in pairs, which is the traditional method of Torah study. In this way, each can be a mirror for the other, reflecting love and respect. But a terrible epidemic invaded the land and all 24,000 students suddenly died, leaving the country spiritually empty for a generation.

To explain what happened, the Talmud states that, "They died because they did not behave respectfully to each other." This is hard to understand, given Rabbi Akiva's holiness and spirituality. Indeed, this was something Rabbi Brandwein could never understand—how, given Rabbi Akiva's purity and spirituality, a lack of respect and caring for one another could bring about the death of his students.

"If even the great Rabbi Akiva's students could be punished in this manner, according to the Talmud, what can we expect for the so-called spiritual people of today?" Rabbi Brandwein would ask, *"What about the average person, who frequently behaves no better than a wild animal?"*

The only remedy for this, my teacher concluded, was the study of the *Zohar*. Only in the *Zohar* did truths exist that could fight the poison of our *Desire to Receive* for the Self Alone. Only the *Zohar* had the power to remold our destructive tendencies into compassion and love.

A few months after Rabbi Brandwein moved to his building in Jerusalem, an incident occurred, which gave him an opportunity to more fully explain these ideas to me. One day, during our studies, a blind man came to my teacher's door. Rabbi Brandwein would often see people from the community, regardless of the reason. His willingness to share both his time and energy with people was unbounded. You hardly needed an appointment with him for it was known that his door was open to all.

Rabbi Brandwein's housekeeper led the man into my teacher's study then left the three of us alone. The man was rather young and well-dressed, but obviously blind. After introducing himself, he groped behind himself for a chair and sat down heavily.

"What can I do for you sir?" Rabbi Brandwein asked politely.

"I have been told you have the power to heal."

Here the young man paused for a moment and then resumed more cautiously: "I would like you to restore my vision, which I lost last year in a terrible factory accident. The doctors have told me there is nothing that can be done, but I know this is not so."

"I do not have the power to heal," Rabbi Brandwein answered. "But it is true The Creator does, and if I so merit it, he will put this power in my hands, for the Light of the Creator is truly nourishing, and can heal even the most estranged. You must agree, however, to one condition. You must promise that if you are truly healed, you will not hate me."

"Why would I ever hate you?" The man looked very surprised. "Such goodness could never be repaid. There would be no possible payment for such a miracle."

"You would hate me because what I had given you was unearned and thus it would cause embarrassment and shame."

The man promised this would not be the case, though Rabbi Brandwein did not look convinced. Nonetheless, he agreed to pray with the man and a short time later the man left. It was some time before I learned what became of his blindness, though I had no doubt in that moment that if The Creator so desired it, Rabbi Brandwein would certainly bring Light into this man's life.

After the man had left, Rabbi Brandwein turned to me: "The chance this man will hate me is real, you know, and I will tell you why. We know from the destruction of the Holy Temple that most people ignore the law of Creation. They do not merit the goodness which is given to them, and therefore, they can only receive Bread of Shame: The pain that always accompanies unearned beneficence if the gifts given to us that are unmerited by our own spiritual work. Good is only enjoyed when a person earns it through hard work and the stronger the effort, the sweeter the taste of the fruit.

"This is the cause of what I call 'hatred for no reason,' a disease which is horribly pronounced among certain individuals because of their great *Desire to Receive*. This gift which they have been given by The Creator, an unusually large spiritual vessel to contain His Light, is a mixed blessing; because it allows them to be filled with His Light, yet at the same time it can block them from true goodness. The larger the vessel is, the more a person might potentially have to give to others, yet, at the same time, the worse his hatred might be if he cannot transform his *Desire to Receive* into a *Desire to Share*. The challenge for such people is to transform their *Desire to Receive* into a *Desire to Share*. If this is not possible, however, the *Desire to Receive* will grow larger and larger until it swallows everything around it, and this unfortunately has been the case for humanity itself over thousands upon thousands of years. Human history is simply a record of self-serving desire run rampant fueled by hatred, envy, distrust. If someone has something we also have, we despise him."

"I am sorry to say this, but it is true. We are ready to swallow each other with our *Desire to Receive*, which is unlike the hunger of wild animals who only devour each other to prolong their existence. *Hatred for no reason is a person's unending hunger for more, even if he is not lacking in anything.* Some might call it greed, but it is much worse than that, and far more dangerous."

THE LIGHT THEREIN WILL RESTORE HIM

My teacher frequently returned to this subject of hatred for no reason, in particular, the hatred we feel for those who have an overpowering *Desire to Receive*, which runs rampant in far too many people. A person with a great *Desire to Receive* can literally seem to want to control the world, and the world will sense this and hate him for it. On the other hand, because the spiritual vessel of such a person is so great, there is the potential to transform the voracious *Desire to Receive* into a *Desire to Share*. When this occurs among a sufficient number of people, then all the world will be blessed with sustenance and plenty—that is, with sharing of the Light—and order will return to all our lives.

But if people with great desire only hoard the Light they have collected, then chaos, doubt, disease and death are the inevitable result. As it has for so long, destruction will prevail in the world. There are many such people, millions of them, and their only real hope for redemption is Kabbalah, for as it is written, "the Light therein will restore [a person] to the right way."

Kabbalah is the only real tool for removing the affliction of *Desire to Receive* for the Self Alone and the spiritual disease that Rabbi Brandwein called hatred for no reason. Rabbi Brandwein taught that use of this tool is simple: Shine the Light on others, and all hatred will disappear, as will all aspects of darkness and negativity in the world.

Unfortunately, too many of us who experience the anger of others want to blame *them* for the problem, rather than search ourselves. To elucidate this problem, Rabbi Brandwein liked to analyze the story of Esau and Jacob from Rashi's commentary on this portion of Vayishalch.

"How would you interpret the story of Esau and Jacob," Rabbi Brandwein once asked me, "in light of this hatred that has no reason?"

Esau and Jacob were twin brothers, of course, yet they were different as night from day. Jacob's life was righteous and full of Light, while Esau was a great criminal, crippled by darkness and envy, especially toward his brother. And this hatred was in fact a tradition or Halachah. Nonetheless, Esau kisses Jacob with all his heart!

Rabbi Brandwein's question to me was complex. Was Esau fulfilling some commandment by hating Jacob? Why was Esau's hatred so profoundly transformed at the end of the story? How was hatred turned into love?

"Well," I began carefully, "as you have told me before, the concept a commandment denotes is a process of obedience, as well as a law or rule. So Esau is more than simply a negative person—he is someone in the process of becoming someone else, just as all are in the process of transformation. Though he is full of darkness and negativity in the beginning, he is actually waiting for the infusion of Light from his brother Jacob, and when it reaches him he cannot help but be transformed, for Light transforms all."

"Very good," answered Rabbi Brandwein. "Of course, the same process can take place among the nations and peoples of the world. We are all transforming. As the energy of the Light reaches us, we respond with only compassion and love. But when we are deprived of the Light, darkness and negativity increase continuously and manifest as pure hatred, particularly against nations or people that we perceive as possessing the Light, or even hoarding it. The people of the world are desperate for Light that is channeled to them from others. When this does not happen, negativity, hatred, and violence are the result."

This discussion also helped me to understand the incident with the blind man. If my teacher of blessed memory had simply restored his sight then and there, he sensed the possibility that the blind man would hate him. Others might not have perceived or foreseen this, certainly the blind man himself had been unaware of it. It did not however escape Rabbi Brandwein and it was for this reason that he warned the blind man: *It was in order to awaken his consciousness.*

A short time before I left Israel, I happened to encounter this man in the street and his sight had indeed been restored. We did not get a chance to visit at length as he was rushing off to an appointment, but he shook my hand with tremendous gratitude, and I could see tears in his eyes.

"I think of Rabbi Brandwein so often," he said. "He restored much more than my sight."

HOW ARE WE TO KNOW WHO IS TRULY SPIRITUAL?

According to the ancient sage known as the Vilna Gaon, the inner wisdom of Kabbalah is sacred, while the literal and external aspects of study are comparatively superficial. As the Gaon puts it, "The chaff is the details of the pronunciation of words, which is the outermost skin of the Torah. In this there is no understanding whatsoever, but only the usage for the words and their pronunciation. Although all of this pertains to the sacredness of the Torah, it is merely an outer shell when compared to the wisdom of Kabbalah."

My teacher frequently arranged for the printing of books on various aspects of Kabbalah. Then he and I would go to the open market of Jerusalem, where we would offer the books to the people, in hopes of bringing them closer to the holiness of The Creator. How wonderful that market was, full of bright stalls and people of all descriptions and the sounds of many languages! Though we attracted quite a few interested shoppers to our stall, a disturbing thought often occurred to me: How could we know whether the individuals who bought our books were truly spiritual people, genuinely prepared to go explore the hidden wisdom of Kabbalah?

One day, as we were setting up our bookstall, I asked Rabbi Brandwein about this, and he set down a stack of books for a moment to answer.

"Of course we may draw people who seem to have little true interest in spirituality," he said, "but of what consequence is this? How is it possible to really know who is spiritual and who is not? Look around you right now. Can you guess with any assurance which of these people leads a truly spiritual life?"

I gazed at the chaotic scene of the marketplace, full of activity on this bright Sunday afternoon. At the stall next to us were Israelis, at the stall beyond Palestinians. Shoppers seemed to be of every possible race and nationality: Americans, Germans, Swedes, even a group of about ten Japanese tourists.

"You see those Japanese over there?" my teacher continued. "It so happens that many years ago a very devout group of Japanese travelers came to me, wanting a teacher in Kabbalah. Many people might find this hard to believe that people from such a different tradition would be drawn to Kabbalah, but I've always known that profound spiritual truth recognizes no boundaries. They asked if I could return to Japan to instruct them, which unfortunately was impossible. I knew they were disappointed, but I also think they were gratified that I'd taken their request seriously. In any case, I didn't feel a need to judge whether they merited the study of Kabbalah."

As the day wore on, all kinds of people stopped

at our stall. A teenage boy stayed for quite a while and bought several books. Toward late afternoon, we began to pack up. As we gathered our things, Rabbi Brandwein resumed the conversation started earlier in the day.

"With the destruction of the Holy Temple, the ten tribes of Israel were dispersed and lost. To this day no one knows where they are, and it's impossible to identify a member of a tribe. The Talmud tells us that only Elijah, in the days of the Messiah, will be able to identify the truly spiritual. Even if we might prefer that our material not be read by non-spiritual people, it is absolutely essential that the message of Kabbalah go out to the world. We should disperse it widely and not worry if it should fall into so called wrong hands. That is not our concern. As I wrote in my prologue to *The Writings of the Ari,* "*It only rests upon us to reveal this holy wisdom. This is our duty.*"

"In the 17th century, Rabbi Avraham Azulai wrote in his book, *Or Hachamah* (Light of the Sun), that there had been a period of time when the open study of Kabbalah was prohibited, but that period ended toward the close of the 15th century. From that time forward, it has been highly desirable for all people to study Kabbalah, since for this reason alone, the Messiah will come."

By now the market crowd was thinning, the sun was much lower in the sky and we began our walk back to Rabbi Brandwein's school. We had sold many of our books and there was only a small box to carry.

"Then how is it possible," I asked, "that 400 years have gone by and in all that time the world as a whole has not discovered Kabbalah, let alone studied it? Even the Rabbis have continued to argue against it."

Rabbi Brandwein did not answer immediately. He thought for a moment and then said, "I have no answer for what you're asking, except to say that, sadly, it is true. *The reason evil grows stronger in the world is the world's failure to study Kabbalah.* As the *Zohar* tells us, *'Woe to those people of closed eyes upon whom it was said, eyes they have, but they cannot see the light of the Torah. They are as beasts who do not see nor know anything else but the straw of the Torah, which is as the husk and the outer part of the wisdom'.*"

As we reached the door of the Rabbi's school, I happened to turn and for a moment I caught a glimpse of the teenage boy who had purchased so many of our books. He had opened one of them and was reading it with great interest, obviously completely absorbed. Whether or not he was "truly spiritual" when he bought the books, he was clearly well on the way to becoming so.

KABBALAH SHOULD BE UNDERSTANDABLE TO EVERYONE

In 1974, the Rabbinit Karen and I published the English translation of Rabbi Brandwein's, *An Introduction to the Book of the Zohar,* and, *An Entrance to the Tree of Life.* I can still remember the day Karen and I brought the order to the printer and how we looked in each other's eyes when we left his shop. We felt blessed beyond measure to have undertaken this important task. *But where would the money come from to pay for the job?*

It was not a small amount, since the books were long and we had requested many copies. In addition, the printer was a friend of ours, and someone we knew to be a worthy individual. We certainly did not want to cheat him of his money—and somehow, when the order was ready two weeks later, the money was there!

This taught us an important lesson. Our obligation is simply to spread the word of Kabbalah. Money for doing so will be provided—and Rabbi Brandwein stressed this again and again. "Have no fear," he would say. "Rabbi Shimon bar Yochai—the author of the *Zohar*—will be with you always, and in his treasury there is an infinite amount of money. Be confident that he will always take good care of you."

As Karen and I drove back to our apartment in Tel Aviv after getting the books from the printer, I thought of a conversation I'd had with Rabbi Brandwein regarding the importance of studying Kabbalah, and the obligation we had to make this possible for as many people as we could.

"Yet Rabbis themselves have argued against this study," I said. "Your own teacher, Rabbi Ashlag, passionately fought for the study of Kabbalah—he knew that only Kabbalah could prevent the disaster in Europe that cost so many millions of lives. Yet no one would listen. To this day, Rabbis and other members of our community are still against opening the wisdom of Kabbalah to everyone. Again and again, we hear the same old objections: We are not yet fit for the study of Kabbalah ... We have not yet the ability to perceive the depth of the wisdom ..."

"Well, we both know that's all nonsense," said Rabbi Brandwein. "People far wiser than us have said so. That's why so many who oppose the study are unable to give a reason—just that it is 'forbidden.' How foolish, and how dangerous! As the Tikunim of the *Zohar* says, '...whatever they [those who study the outer aspects of the Torah only] do is for their own benefit alone, and they do not give a thought for the general welfare of others'."

"There is no other solution to the dangers that surround us," he continued. "Kabbalah must be made understandable to the common person. It is imperative that Israel and all the nations of the world find their way to Kabbalah. The time has come when those who are alienated from spirituality must at last return, and only through Kabbalah this is possible."

This is why Rabbi Brandwein and I worked so hard to publish the first part of Rabbi Ashlag's *Ten Luminous Emanations* in English. We had a duty to spread the wisdom of Kabbalah, my teacher said. He warned that opposition to our effort would become stronger over time, and that I myself would be criticized and slandered in the future. But he counseled me to always rise above this, for my path was the correct one.

The great scholar and Kabbalist Rabbi Moshe Cordovero once wrote, "Whoever causes the removal of the wisdom of Kabbalah and the inner wisdom from both the Oral and Written Torahs, and causes people to refrain from studying—it is as though he has cut off the flow from the river Zeir Anpin, and from its garden, the Malchut. Woe to him, for it would be better if he had not been created in this world."

Rabbi Brandwein emphasized that such people had been present since the days of Moses, and their only goal was the spread of darkness. "But I promise that the Creator will protect you in your work of spreading the Light of Kabbalah and the *Zohar*. It is not even necessary to notice your enemies, who are after all only temporary. They are like thorns, that are here one day and gone the next."

From a Kabbalistic perspective, no tendency is more spiritually self-destructive than the impulse to feel hatred and enmity toward another human being. This is made very clear in the *Zohar* through a discussion of those who choose to see Noah from a negative perpective. The inclination to see negativity in anyone, particularly a patriarch such as Noah, is itself extremely corrosive. For the sake of our own souls rather than those on whom we choose to pass judgment, cleansing ourselves of this negative inclination must be part of our transformation.

"THE MIKVEH CONTAINS ALL THE SECRETS OF LIFE"

If there is one thing I truly believe I inherited from Rabbi Brandwein, it is his way of behaving in the world—the way he conducted himself day in and day out. I thank G-d for this, and I sense it is true because of the hundreds of thousands of people we have been able to draw back to spirituality. Like Rabbi Brandwein, I have only been motivated by my desire to bring Kabbalah to the common person. Those who hate me—as they hated Rabbi Brandwein—continue to be driven by anger, money and position, but I know that slowly even the strength of their hatred will diminish. The only difference between myself and Rabbi Brandwein is that while he worked alone, I have been aided by my family, by many students, and by a large, multinational congregation.

Rabbi Brandwein was the first to stand up to the religious traditionalists, who believed that people must study and worship in only one way. Underlying this viewpoint of so-called religious people there is may be a certain visceral discomfort at even being in the presence of the non-religious—and it may be possible that my teacher too felt this to some extent. With his beard and side-locks, he must have known that he looked strange to many people. But Rabbi Brandwein never let this get in the way of his mission. His only goal was to spread love in the deepest and most holy sense. Few so-called religious people genuinely "love their neighbors," but my teacher clearly understood his *tikun*—the correction and restitution of his soul—and therefore his purpose in life was clear.

This concept of *tikun* is absolutely fundamental to Kabbalistic teaching. In the *Zohar*, this is clearly and elucidated through the Torah narratives of Abraham and Sarah. Each of us comes into the world with aspects of our character that may seem to be immutable, but that are in fact within our power to change, though only with difficulty. Abraham and Sarah were seemingly destined to be childless, but they transcended this fate through their trust in the Creator and the difficult spiritual work they accomplished. Each of our lives contains an essential paradox: Our destiny is already known to the Creator, but we have the power and free will to alter it. Whether we do so in this lifetime, or not for many yet to come, is a choice each of us has to make.

Hatred, obsession with money, struggle for power—these three forces of darkness have existed since the time of Cain and Abel, and our only solution to them is love. Only love can bring truth. For all the success we have had in the United States and around the world, I remain permanently grateful to my teacher, and his teacher before him, Rabbi Ashlag. Without their help, we would be nothing at all.

I am sure there were many traditional people who privately admitted the truth of what Rabbi Brandwein was saying, yet they continued to hate him publicly because they were jealous of what he was accomplishing. They couldn't stand that he had won the love and admiration of so many secular people.

A good example of Rabbi Brandwein's open attitude toward the common person concerned the hotel swimming pool, mentioned earlier. He was happy about the pool, because he knew that dipping in it could be considered immersion in a *mikveh*. "The *mikveh* contains all the secrets of life," he told me once. "It can cure disease, even cancer, and of course greatly enhance the process of healing."

At the time, I did not completely understand this comment, but I listened to him carefully. "For instance, the *mikveh* used by the Holy Ari, Rabbi Luria over 500 years ago, is still considered a place of great importance, and people draw water from it to put into other *mikvaot*. Even a drop of the water can add holiness."

Listening to him talk suddenly reminded me of a time when I lived in a town with over 700 religious families, and only three of them made use of the *mikveh*, which was always incredible to me. How could so many so-called spiritual people ignore this great blessing of The Creator?

"Here," he continued, "look at this letter from Rabbi Ashlag that he sent to his uncle so many years ago. This is a copy that I made in my own handwriting, and I've kept it for many years."

Rabbi Brandwein opened a drawer of his desk and withdrew a frail piece of paper. The desk was very large and at least a hundred years old. It had many small drawers and cabinets, and it was easy to imagine that it contained all the wisdom of the world. The paper was already yellowed and frayed, but obviously cherished. He handed it to me and I began to read:

Dear Uncle... the letter began.

It was amazing to actually be reading a letter from Rabbi Ashlag! This is what closeness to my teacher often brought—a chance to feel the connection in the great lineage of Kabbalah.

The letter continued, *"Just today my teacher has taught me a great and comprehensive secret concerning a certain mikveh in his community that was measured and found lacking. I have been informed that we are going to work to replenish the waters of the mikveh, for as it is said, these waters contain all the secrets of life. I was over my head with joy as you can imagine..."*

"While you think you may understand this letter, you can not fully grasp its significance," Rabbi Brandwein warned, "because you do not fully understand the importance of the *mikveh*. This is not a problem, however. You will achieve understanding over time. The secret of the *mikveh*, like all great subjects of Kabbalah, requires years of study. You will come to cherish its mysterious, healing powers, and the truth which resides at its essence. Remember that all life flows from the springs of The Creator, and all can be healed as well. For as it is said, "I will sprinkle clean water upon you and you shall be clean.""

THE TEN LUMINOUS EMANATIONS

During my time with Rabbi Brandwein, I learned other secrets as well, and none more important than in my study of the *Ten Luminous Emanations*. When I first began studying this book, my teacher suggested that I visit another eminent Rabbi for aid and instruction, since he had also been a student of Rabbi Ashlag. It was unclear to me at the time why my teacher sent me to study with this person, but I was happy to go, as all of Rabbi Brandwein's instructions proved useful in one way or another. I should add that during this period I was studying the second part of the *Ten Luminous Emanations*, which concerns wisdom. Here, Rabbi Ashlag examines the contemplative aspects of God's thought, and the unknowable point of creation from which all knowable reality originates.

My work on the *Ten Luminous Emanations* was proceeding well when I visited the Rabbi to whom my techer had referred me. As I expected, he asked me which section I was studying, and whether I had reached the fifth part, which dealt with judgment and power. This was the most difficult section, he said, and perhaps I should skip over it. Most people did not study it at all.

When Rabbi Brandwein heard this, however, he vigorously disagreed. True, the fifth part was difficult, but without it one could never reach a full understanding of Rabbi Ashlag's ideas without it. In fact, I had better begin the study of it immediately, and in a group if at all possible. "Group study," said Rabbi Brandwein, "allows for much greater understanding than what anyone can achieve alone."

Years later, in America, I put my teacher's very sound advice into practice. In 1994, I was privileged to teach the fifth part of the *Ten Luminous Emanations* to many groups of students. This was the first time this had been attempted since Rabbi

Brandwein's edition of the book appeared in 1969. Our group study continues to this day and has brought greater understanding of Kabbalah—and even the nature of reality itself—to many people. Often, after our study of a particular chapter, we will reflect on the continuing discoveries of quantum physics, which confirm exactly what the Holy Ari said so long ago. In a circuitous way, modern physicists are retracing the philosophical steps taken by Kabbalists almost 400 years ago. On a less abstract level, study of the fifth part of *Ten Luminous Emanations*, which deals as it does with so many central questions of life, has helped to bring thousands and to a deeper level of spirituality.

I hope that I have fulfilled my teacher's wishes for me when he stated that I was the one person who could explain the *Ten Luminous Emanations* to the world at large. I've worked diligently toward that purpose. With the help of The Creator, may this holy mission that I accepted from Rabbi Brandwein continue to awaken many people to their spiritual roots.

TO PAY IN ADVANCE FOR A FUTURE DEBT

Rabbi Brandwein once told me that when a person borrows a sum of money, the lender will accept collateral as a kind of debt insurance, but the lender still wants to be paid back. This should be obvious—but in many areas of life we assume collateral by itself is sufficient and that we can walk away from what we owe to others.

Our discussion about debt came up during a trip to Safed and Meron to visit the burial sites of the righteous. Rabbi Brandwein's father had a piece of mortgaged property in Safed, but he had died before he could pay off what he owed. After visiting the cemeteries of the Tzadikim in Safed, we drove out to this property, which was a small piece of run-down land on the edge of a suburb. The surrounding villages were rather pleasant, but it was clear no one had cared for his father's property in many years. There was a run-down house, and the ground was overgrown with weeds.

"Come," Rabbi Brandwein said, "let's take a walk."

We began walking along the edge of the lot, among the yellowed grass and wildflowers.

"My father bought this house many years ago, but never managed to fix it up as he had hoped. He owned it free and clear, but near the end of his life he needed quite a bit of extra money for medical care, so he borrowed against it. Unfortunately, he was never able to pay off his debt, and it's been vacant ever since. Perhaps the lender tried to sell it himself, but this area of Safed is not very popular. I brought you out here to see it because we were in the area, and also to ask you a great favor. The other night, my father came to me in a dream and told me that somehow the debt on this property must be paid off."

Rabbi Brandwein's voice was gentle, but I could see his will was firm.

"When I woke," he continued, "I couldn't get the dream out of my head. I even called the lender, who told me the exact amount that was owed. As you know we have little money, and what we do have, must be put to the publications of our books and our educational projects. So I would like to ask you to pay the debt. When you do, the property will be transferred into your name."

I thought for a moment or two, but knew of course that I would say yes. What I did not understand at the time, however, was why a loan which was backed-up by collateral would need to be paid off in the first place. Why didn't the lender simply take the collateral for himself? I also did not fully understand why Rabbi Brandwein had chosen me to pay back the debt.

It was then that my teacher informed me that

lenders were less interested in property than in having their debts resolved, and his father had been so firm in the dream, so perhaps there were other reasons as well.

Walking back to the car that day, a new question occurred to me: Was there some connection between myself and the debt Rabbi Brandwein's father had left behind? Was there a reason why I was privileged to perform this deed?

"Those are excellent questions," he replied. "In life, there are endless connections between seemingly disconnected events. This particular connection is unclear to you at this time, but one day you will fully understand why you are being given the responsibility of paying the debt. If you like, you can think of it as paying one of your own debts in advance, because that's what you're really doing. You never knew my father and had no connection to him, yet you are performing an act of great good will, and this will be repaid.

"In life we are sometimes given an opportunity to do this, to perform a good deed in advance for a future obligation. Heaven gives us this privilege, and when the time comes for us to pay back our obligation, a debt owing from a past life, perhaps this will not be necessary. The repayment has already been accomplished."

The next day we went to his father's lender and I wrote a check, clearing the debt entirely. Rabbi Brandwein's father could not thank me in person, but I felt his gratitude nonetheless. At the time, I could not fully understand the significance of what I had done, but I knew it would be revealed at some point in my future. The day would come when an obligation would be asked of me, and my debt would already be paid.

My teacher of blessed memory foresaw all the events of my future life, and made sure that I was well taken care of!

NEVER FORGET YOU WERE CHOSEN TO SERVE THE PUBLIC

When someone asked Rabbi Brandwein for a favor, my teacher's very first thought was always, *"Why not do this kindness?"* rather than a negative response like, *"Why should I bother?"* or, *"What's in it for me?"* He had a reputation as someone who liked to help others, therefore people often came to him with appeals both large and small. There was one request, however, that even I doubted if Rabbi Brandwein could satisfy, not for lack of effort, but because the people involved were so diametrically opposed to one another.

The request was made by the Sepharadic community of Safed, for a Rabbi from their own community. The term Sepharadic refers to Hebrews of Mediterranean descent who lived (or still live) in the lands surrounding the Mediterranean after the exile from the Holy Land. On the other hand, those who lived in Eastern Europe came to be called Ashkenazi. These two groups lived in such different areas over the centuries that their cultures are very different. Even their languages are different, and while there isn't overt conflict between the two groups, there can be segregation and even animosity.

Generally speaking, the dominant political class in Israel has been Ashkenazi. For many years, Safed had been almost entirely Sepharadic, but more recently the area had been heavily populated by the Ashkenazi, and they controlled most of the important institutions. The Sephardic community in Safed did not even have their own Rabbi.

It was for this reason that a group of Sepharadic residents came to Rabbi Brandwein with their request. While Rabbi Brandwein himself was of Ashkenazi descent, they knew he would treat them fairly. The town's Ashkenazi Rabbi was a good man, they said, but he did not understand the hearts and minds of the Sepharadic community. They wanted a Rabbi of their own and asked Rabbi Brandwein to help them accomplish this.

When I initially heard the request, I did not have much hope. The religious council of Safed was over-whelmingly Ashkenazi and the council had substantial political clout. I thought to myself, "The Sepharadim have less chance of getting a Separadic Rabbi than Moses had when he parted the Red Sea!"

But I underestimated the persuasive power of my teacher. The Sepharadim wanted a young rabbi by the name of Rabbi Dayan and Rabbi Brandwein agreed to help. "I will put all my energy to it," he promised, "and with my friends and acquaintances, we will see what can be done."

As it happened, two-thirds of all the members of the religious councils in the entire state of Israel were connected to the Mapai, the party then in power in the central government. Both the Mapai, as well as all the members of the Workers' Union, knew that if Rabbi Brandwein suggested something, it was worth getting done. For this reason they agreed, and a Sepharadic Rabbinate was established in Safed.

When he reported the victory to the group of Sepharadim who had made the request, he was very serious. For Rabbi Dayan, this was his first assignment. "Never forget," Rabbi Brandwein told him, "that you have been chosen as Head Rabbi of the Sepharadic community to serve the people only. I am trusting you that you will not get involved in politics, even a little bit. You must dedicate all of your time and effort to public service. I am speaking to the Sepharadic citizens gathered here as well. Do not pressure him in this."

Rabbi Brandwein frequently agreed to help with favors and requests, but this was probably the occasion that required the greatest effort and skill. The high government officials did not like change. They followed the 'party-line' without thinking further. Rabbi Brandwein received many warnings during this time, both friendly and unfriendly from people who did not want him to do anything on behalf of the Sepharadic community. "If you are a true Ashkenazi," they said, "you will do nothing."

But, of course, that was not my Rabbi's way.

MONEY IS MERELY A MEDIUM FOR SPREADING KABBALAH

Shortly after I began studying with Rabbi Brandwein, a Rabbi from another town telephoned to ask if my teacher would help him get a job koshering the kitchen of a certain Histradut factory. Around the time Rabbi Brandwein had been involved with koshering the kitchens of several Histradut factories, including a very large one in Cholon, so he had gained a reputation for doing this.

But Rabbi Brandwein's written reply to this particular request was unequivocal. His only purpose in koshering factory kitchens was drawing people back to their spirituality. But this was not a job, it was a labor of love, so he would have to decline the request. He would not intervene to help this individual gain a paying position koshering kitchens. "The only purpose of money," he wrote, "is in the good it can do for others". I later heard that the Rabbi was surprised by Rabbi Brandwein's response, but my teacher was adamant.

On the occasions that Rabbi Brandwein himself was given money, he was also extremely scrupulous, particularly with money from public funds. He was well known for this. Once he went to the Histradut management to ask for money to print an edition of the *Hashmatot HaZohar*, or Omissions of the *Zohar*. With no questions asked, they gladly handed over a very large amount for printing costs.

The donation was given with no strings attached, for Rabbi Brandwein to use as he saw fit.

Although no one ever investigated how the money was spent, all of it went into the printing project, without even a lira left over for his own personal expenses. At the time, someone mentioned to him that 3,000 liras or so would have been a very reasonable salary, but he wouldn't hear of it.

It is so rare nowadays, to find a person as concerned with another's money as they are with their own, but that was how Rabbi Brandwein was. Of course, the Rabbi who had telephoned him for the job could never understand this, but my teacher's only purpose in life was to spread the wisdom of Kabbalah. "Those who have been alienated from their spirituality must once again be allowed to taste the inner truth of the Torah," he said. "Money is merely a medium for spreading Kabbalah. It is nothing more."

THE TREASURY OF RABBI SHIMON

Kabbalists have always been short of money. This is a simple fact. Rabbi Shmuel Vital, whose father studied with the great Rabbi Isaac Luria, wrote about this fact and so did many others after him. Rabbi Brandwein's own teacher, Rabbi Ashlag, once wanted to publish an encyclopedia of all the concepts and terminologies of Kabbalah, but this tremendous idea was stopped in its tracks for lack of funds. In my own publication enterprises, I have never known beforehand where the money would come from, but as Rabbi Brandwein always assured me, my work on Kabbalah would be provided for, and this in fact has been the case. When we decided to publish books at the Kabbalah Centre, for example, the money appeared exactly when needed it, so that we never once fell behind in our payments to the printer. And this was also the case in each of the publications which I worked on with Rabbi Brandwein.

Our initial project together was an English translation of the first part of the *Ten Luminous Emanations*, and after that *Likutei Torah*, or *Compilations*, which is the 12th volume of *The Writings of the Ari*. Again, at no time in our work together did we consider where the money would come from, yet the required funds always appeared when we needed them.

Praised be to The Creator, this has continued to be the case for over 30 years in all my publishing enterprises. When I have endeavored to print the word of The Creator, money has been given to us, as it is to all true Kabbalists. In the same way, when we are able, we have helped others in their work, as befits those whose faith lies in the *Zohar*.

There was one Rabbi, for example, whose books I myself sold in the United States to help pay for his printing costs. His name was Rabbi Yosef Weinstock, and he had been a student of Rabbi Ashlag. He had printed a full, 21-volume set of the *Zohar*, along with Rabbi Ashlag's most famous work *The Sulam*, which is a commentary on the *Zohar*. The commentary itself filled ten volumes, though in a small format. It was Rabbi Weinstock's opinion that this essential material should be available as pocket-size books.

Rabbi Weinstock had already printed 1,000 sets of the *Zohar* in London when he contacted Rabbi Brandwein. Unfortunately, they were not selling as well as expected. My teacher immediately ordered 50 volumes for the Histradut, and I ordered 700 sets for the United States. At the time, I was not sure how I would pay for them, but I obtained a list of all the Rabbis in the country, and began selling ten volumes at the price of $20 to each Rabbi. This was quite a discount as in 1965, the cost of printing such a set was $50. But, praise be to The Creator, through the efforts of Rabbi Weinstock and myself, this was the first time the Kabbalah was widely studied in the United States.

At about this time, Rabbi Brandwein's translation of the *Hashmatot HaZohar* was also completed, and though the Histradut management had funded the printing, we now needed to sell it. Unfortunately, few people in Israel were interested in buying Rabbi Brandwein's books, so we took a thousand volumes and managed to sell them in the United States. Although hardly anyone who bought them could even read the *Zohar*, this was an important beginning. I could not begin to imagine all that would take place in the future, my teacher's vision and the full impact that teaching Kabbalah would have on so many people. Only 20 years after Rabbi Brandwein struggled to sell the *Hashmatot HaZohar*, we began publishing a magnificent edition of the *Zohar* together with *The Sulam*. Each batch of the printing comprised 25,000 books and we have had many interested customers.

Rabbi Brandwein once told me that those who dedicate their lives to the spreading of Kabbalah will always be short of money. This is simply a truth that can not be denied, and yet our wealth will surely lie elsewhere, so that none of us will have reason to complain. Another person involved in such work might ask the Holy One, blessed be He, why He does not provide greater assistance? But the true Kabbalist understands that this question is irrelevant. If the account below is smaller than might be hoped for, he knows the coffers will be filled to overflowing in the realms above.

It is a Kabbalistic principle that whatever is manifest in the physical world is inherently less powerful than what remains hidden or invisible. The *Zohar*, therefore, attaches little importance to worldly wealth or success or if a person is poor in a material sense for there is an inference that wealth of a higher form awaits in the Upper Worlds. A discourse on the Book of Job provides a good example of the *Zohar's* view of the complex relationship between material wealth and spiritual well-being and of the frequent need to detach from one in order to gain the other. Yet there is no need to be scornful of wealth in itself. *The danger is not in riches, but in the temptations and the destructive forms of consciousness that it may create.*

TROUBLE AND PROBLEMS ARE ALWAYS PART OF "THE PROCESS"

Rabbi Brandwein of blessed memory taught that all the problems we encounter in achieving worthy goals are vital to the process of our development as human beings. "There is no question," he often said, "that the holy Light desires only good for all people. Light knows no other way. Problems will arise to block your path, yet this is only to test your faith in the blessed Creator. Heaven forbid that we begin to doubt!

"It will probably be many years before you see the fruits of our endeavor together, our project of bringing the wisdom of Kabbalah to the common person," Rabbi Brandwein would say, "and there will be more years when you will work alone. But you must take no notice of this. What occurs during the process of your development is unimportant to its end. When the time is right, what should happen, will happen. Never forget this."

Thinking back over more than three decades, it is true that the process of bringing Kabbalah to the general public was slow at first, and we had many struggles. But I have always remembered what Rabbi Brandwein said, and taken his words to heart. In the 1960s and 1970s, most people had never even heard of Kabbalah, and few had any interest in the kind of books we were publishing. To continue printing books, we needed a great deal of money, and often there was a negative balance. It would have been easy to lose faith in our vision, but since Rabbi Brandwein had told me so clearly that these problems were simply part of the process, they hardly troubled us at all.

Before Rabbi Brandwein's death, he and I succeeded in selling all the small sets of the *Zohar* published by Rabbi Weinstock, our printing of the *Hashmatot HaZohar,* and all our copies of The Tikunim of the *Zohar.* In addition, we were able to interest people in Rabbi Brandwein's *Ma'alot Hasulam,* or *The Rungs of the Ladder,* which was a commentary on *The Sulam* of Rabbi Ashlag, together with the remaining copies of *The Writings of the Ari,* printed by my teacher in 1960. By 1965, barely 100 sets of this last book had been sold, so Rabbi Brandwein asked me to take the remainder and distribute them at a discount around the world. Of course, the Kabbalah Centre in the United States took them. While we did not give them away for free, we sold them at a much reduced cost, as Rabbi Brandwein requested.

In 1969, just a few months before Rabbi Brandwein's death, he and I finalized the contract for a second printing of *The Writings of the Ari.* This was something that took me many years to understand— why Rabbi Brandwein elected to print another edition of a book that had been so difficult to sell in the first place. Nevertheless, I did not argue with my teacher's request. "It is necessary to continue the process," he said, "regardless of what kind response we sense at this time. No one can argue that this is not an essential work. Its value will be recognized over time."

When the volumes were printed, interest was again slow, though they sold steadily over the next decade. Then, in 1983, I unexpectedly had a strong feeling that my wife, the Rabbinit Karen, and I should print *The Writings of the Ari* as a complete 18-volume set. Actually, it was more than just a strong feeling; it was a kind of inspiration, and I personally had no doubt that it was a message from Rabbi Brandwein himself. At this point we had established our Centre in the United Sates, we were just getting on our feet, and we did not have a great deal of funds. Naturally, I was a bit uneasy about such an idea. It had taken nearly 20 years to sell the 1,000 sets of the same work which Rabbi Brandwein initially printed in 1960. This new edition would require a great deal of money and judging by past interest, there was no guarantee of a response. It seemed more prudent to print small runs of one volume at a time, moving onto the next volume only when the last one sold out.

Rabbanit Karen, however, strongly disagreed. "If you are going to print *The Writings of the Ari*, you must print the entire series," she said. My wife has a gentle wisdom that is difficult to ignore. "I am confident that Rabbi Brandwein will make sure there are people to buy them. What has to happen, will happen. The time is clearly ripe for this part of the process."

The Rabbanit was right. I followed my wife's suggestion and to date we have printed and sold tens of thousands of sets of *The Writings of the Ari*. Publication of these books greatly benefited the growth of the Centre.

Now, I also understand why Rabbi Brandwein desired to print part of this work before his death. He knew that beginning the process would start a great chain of events that would eventually end in overwhelming success. Something very similar has happened with the *Zohar*, of which we have now printed more than one and a half million volumes, along with the *Ma'alot Hasulam* and the *Sulam* commentaries. Certainly this is what Rabbi Brandwein was aiming for when he began printing the *Zohar* and *The Writings of the Ari*. He was allowing for the unfolding of future events. We ceased our publication of Rabbi Weinstock's smaller versions of the *Zohar* only when we realized that people wanted larger print, but interest in the work itself has grown.

Rabbi Brandwein was happy to work on publishing projects not directly related to Kabbalah, so long as they increased the spiritual awareness of the public in some way. "Millions of people are estranged from the life of the spirit," he would say, "and not drawing any closer at all. Whatever we can do to help is essential." But he often reminded me that it is only through the Tree of Life—that is, through the *Zohar*—that complete redemption will ever come about.

From a Kabbalistic perspective, the familiar story of the trees in the Garden of Eden is a depiction of two very distinct realities. The Tree of Life represents a dimension unlimited by time and space, and untouched by conflict, disease, and death. Through their temptation by the serpent and their sin in eating the fruit of the Tree of Knowledge, Adam and Eve experienced a change in spiritual consciousness that separated them—and us—from the Tree of Life. *Their transgression brought us to the physical world and the level of consciousness that we now inhabit. The essential task of every person, and of humanity in general, is to bring about the spiritual transformation that will reconnect us with the Tree of Life reality.*

My teacher once suggested that we use the funds allotted to us by the Workers' Union to help another Rabbi in preparing a Hebrew translation of the Talmud. My teacher knew that without this money such a translation would be impossible and he even asked me to take some money from our fund in the United States to help with the Talmud project.

"But you've told me many times," I said, "that only through of the Tree of Life will redemption come about. The fact is also, we know there are many others who will finance this publication of the Talmud, while few will finance study of Kabbalah. Wouldn't it be better to save our funds for this purpose, especially considering the many problems we have encountered in our work and are likely to have in the future?"

Rabbi Brandwein gave an answer that only a Kabbalist would give. "It is essential to use any means possible to draw people closer to spirituality," he said. "While it is a fact that in the days preceding the return of the Messiah, only the *Zohar* will redeem us, we must be willing to help in all efforts to distribute spiritual materials, even works not directly related to Kabbalah. Problems and trouble? I don't give them a second thought. This is just part of the process."

I have no doubt that our great success in spreading the wonderful wisdom of the *Zohar*, *The Writings of the Ari*, and the truth of Kabbalah in general is due solely to Rabbi Brandwein's deep belief and enthusiasm for this effort. Hundreds of thousands of people reading our books today had not even heard of Kabbalah 20 years ago. We have come a long way indeed.

THE SEPHARADIC TRADITION MUST BE STRENGTHENED

For cleansing the soul, one hour's worth of studying Kabbalah is equivalent to a year's reading of Torah. The inner aspect of the words of our Creator are much stronger, and until we merit complete redemption, only the books of Kabbalah can help us. *From the evidence of daily life, it is clear we have no alternative. If we forget this, great destructive forces will be unleashed upon the world.*

We have only to look at modern history to see the truth of this. Much of the Jewish community in Europe abandoned the study of Kabbalah in the last century, and, as recently as 1936, Rabbi Yehuda Ashlag warned that because of this, a great cloud of darkness would descend on them. How horribly real that warning became. The Sepharadic community, however, has always been slower to relinquish the inner aspect of the Torah. Many in the Sepharadic community have continued to embrace Kabbalah.

The subject of Sepharadic Kabbalah came up once with Rabbi Brandwein when we were visiting the first branch of the academy he had established in the southern Israeli town of Ofakim. It is a comparatively poor town. In addition, many Tunisians

EDUCATION OF A KABBALIST

and Ethiopians have settled there, ethnically different from the larger population of Israel.

As we arrived in this arid, desert-like community, I asked Rabbi Brandwein why he had established the first branch of his academy so far from Tel Aviv. It was at least a two-hour drive by car, and to be frank, much of the town looked more Arab than Israeli. If he wanted to spread the word of Kabbalah, wasn't there a more accessible location?

"Why did you first target the Tunisian settlers," I continued. "Why not the Ashkenazi, like yourself? I know you have always felt strongly about promoting Kabbalah study, but surely there must have been a closer town."

My teacher's reply surprised me. "Do you remember the Minister of Communication," he said, "Israel Yeshayahu? He stressed the notion that the Sepharadic community should be especially targeted for education in Kabbalah, and I agree with him strongly. Of all the peoples in the Hebrew tradition, this group has continued to hold onto their Kabbalistic roots. Unfortunately, that now is changing. Western ideas and Western technology, have taken over everywhere, and the Sepharadic community is not immune. Some Sepharadic Rabbis are even starting to favor so-called modern spiritual practices. The Moroccan Rabbis, for example, have westernized and no longer even study the *Zohar*. But the Tunisian community is still involved with Kabbalah, and for this reason we must make every effort to support and strengthen them. The Tree of Life is literally the only hope for the world, and the Light of that study still burns within this community."

He spoke with so much feeling, and I suddenly realized why he had warned Rabbi Dayan against any involvement in politics. The young Rabbi would be accepting the spiritual leadership of the Sepharadic community in Safed, and clearly his duty was a sacred one.

During my stay in Israel, I saw too much evidence of the darkness that occurs when that study is forgotten—the dissension between the Sepharadic and Ashkenazi communities and the political dissension within the State of Israel itself. The spiritual person's only true defense against negativity is involvement with the inner aspect of the Torah. This is especially true for those people whose vessels are largest and who therefore, receive the most Light. Without reflecting it back onto the world, they will only bring darkness and destruction to all of us.

Rabbi Brandwein often said that the way spiritual people behave with each other will determine how the rest of the world will treat us. During the destruction of the First and Second Holy Temples, the whole world suffered. After the destruction, no peace was left in the entire world and in fact, this problem remains to this very day. The spiritual among us—those who, according to Rabbi Brandwein, could have stopped the destruction—only kept to the sidelines and did not take responsibility for stabilizing the world. It is surely the duty and obligation of every spiritual man or woman to bring peace to the world, and this can only be done through the study of Kabbalah.

WE MUST NEVER FORGET THE GOOD OF OTHERS

According to the *Zohar*, the judgment of our souls is enacted by the souls themselves. After death, souls return to the Garden of Eden and there they make some important decisions about the future. Some may choose to return to the world in order to accomplish their spiritual correction. Others are entitled to enter paradise. Still other souls may decide to undergo a period of punishment or purgation. The *Zohar* teaches that we are fully in control and responsible for what becomes of us, even after death. There is also a strong implication that we shouldn't wait until we're back in the Garden of Eden to begin exercising this control and responsibility. The *Bible*, the *Zohar*, and the entire Kabbalistic tradition are intended as a highly practical, albeit encoded, set of instructions for improving our lives in the deepest sense. Ultimately, the judgment rendered us will depend on how well we have understood those instructions and put them to use.

It is human nature to judge people according to the good they have done for us today, weighed against any misdeeds of the past. Our final judgment is a combination of the good and bad. This sounds rational, but according to Rabbi Brandwein it is rarely trustworthy for the good that others do far outshines the negative. If a man or woman does a favor for us, we must never forget it—and certainly we should not criticize them for their less than perfect actions at another time.

Rabbi Brandwein often told a story about a rather well-known journalist who had helped him become the Head Rabbi of the Histradut. This man was famous both for his sharp tongue and his political influence. If he did not like you he could "finish you off," so to speak, through his prominent weekly column in a national newspaper. As it is said, the pen is mightier than the sword, and this writer had a great deal of might.

He came from a seventh-generation, well-respected Jerusalem family, but at this time in his life he was not religious at all, and felt very cut off from his spiritual roots. Perhaps this is the reason he approached Rabbi Brandwein. In any case, he appeared one day during the hours that my teacher often saw visitors and suggested the idea that Rabbi Brandwein become the Head Rabbi of the Histradut.

"I am not a religious man," he told Rabbi Brandwein. "To be frank, I have no religious interest at all. However, I want to inform you that this position may be available and certainly the religious members of the Histradut deserve a decent Rabbi."

Rabbi Brandwein was initially surprised to hear such an offer, particularly from such a non-spiritual man of such political influence. "Is the need for a Rabbi so sudden," answered Rabbi Brandwein, "that you would make a special trip out to my house? Why now? I will not hide my surprise."

"No, the need is not sudden, but I believe it exists. As to the trip out to your house, perhaps I would not have made a special trip, but I was in the area and I thought it worth my while to tell you."

Rabbi Brandwein was silent a moment. "What you say is quite interesting. I will not deny that. For one thing, such a position would allow me to bring great goodness to hundreds of thousands of people. However, it is very difficult to imagine that the Po'el Hamizrachi party, the ultra–orthodox religious party in Israel, would even allow the Histradut to have their own Rabbi, since most of their members are professed atheists. This would cause a huge schism. Right now my life is that of a peaceful scholar. Yet spreading the ideas of Kabbalah and spirituality is worth of any degree of conflict, so long as there is a willing audience.

"Don't worry," the journalist said. "I have decided that this is for the best. If others start rumors about you or cause conflict, I will be able to silence them. Believe me, your participation will not cause harm to the public. Rather, it will bring much needed unity."

With these assurances, Rabbi Brandwein decided to accept the position; of course, he never regretted it. He knew that becoming the Rabbi of a non-religious organization would enable him to bring people closer to their spiritual roots. This was worth whatever effort it required.

"This journalist was a man I grew to both respect and suspect," Rabbi Brandwein would say. "As a writer, he at times went too far, and one might argue that he had too much power. Nonetheless, you must never forget the good deeds a person has done for you, regardless of their other actions. Even though this journalist professed a complete lack of spirituality, I believe a deeper part of him was calling out for a connection to his inner spirit. This is what led him to make his offer in the first place."

Over the years, I have found that the favors we receive from others are essential in more than one respect. True, we may be able to struggle on without the help of other people, *but we still must cherish the good that is offered to us.* Though people who have helped us in the past may later turn away from us, this is no reason to forget their good deeds. Quelling our anger can be difficult. Too many of us react from disappointment before we exhibit self-restraint, but if one wants to be a Kabbalist, the appreciation of the good in others is an essential first step. Sadly, this is what the world still lacks, and why studying Kabbalah is so very important.

THE IMPORTANCE OF OUR PAST LIVES

As we've discussed, every human being has a spiritual correction that must be accomplished. Until that *tikun* is completed, our souls will continue to return to the world in new incarnations. The *Zohar* teaches that humanity's collective *tikun* was very nearly completed at the foot of Mount Sinai after the escape from Egypt. However, the Golden Calf incident erased that opportunity. Today, we are closer than ever to eliminating death from the world. Kabbalists assert that the *Zohar* is much more than a description of that soon-to-be-realized miracle. The *Zohar* is a tool for bringing it about and reading the *Zohar* with a pure heart is *using* that tool to best effect.

I once invited the chief Sepharadic Rabbi of Tel Aviv, Rabbi Chayim David Ha-Levi, to give a lecture on reincarnation. At the time it was generally believed that the subject of reincarnation was far outside the bounds of traditional spiritual practice. Reincarnation, however, is an important topic in the *Zohar* and Kabbalistic sages devoted attention to the subject for hundreds of years.

This was in the late 1970s, a few years after Rabbi Brandwein's death., and we were beginning to publish *The Gate of Reincarnation* from *The Writings of the Ari.*

Most of the people in the audience that night paid careful attention to Rabbi Ha-Levi and asked thoughtful questions, which might not have occurred just a few years earlier. Perhaps the idea of reincarnation was beginning to be taken more seriously. Rabbi Yaakov Zohar, whom I met in the vestibule after the talk, told me about a very different reception that was given to Rabbi Ha-Levi at a previous lecture. On that occasion, he was speaking to a group of Rabbis in the city and in the middle of the lecture much of the audience began laughing out loud. To say they were rude would be an understatement, but this is how people reacted at the time to the subject of reincarnation, regardless of the importance it had been accorded in the Rabbinic tradition for hundreds of years.

The widespread interest in reincarnation today is proof again of Rabbi Brandwein's belief that holding to worthy beliefs and goals will eventually be brought to light. "In fact," Rabbi Brandwein would say, "the mere fact that so many disagree with you is often, in itself, proof of the essential validity of your ideas."

I have personally always believed that not taking reincarnation seriously is illogical. This leads to something else Rabbi Brandwein often discussed, which he called the rule of opposites. "If everyone says a particular thing," he would say, "we need to doubt the statement at the very least. Similarly, if something is considered important, we should question it. *And if an idea is not fully accepted by a group, then we need to realize that this idea is probably very significant."*

As I left the synagogue that night after Rabbi Ha-Levi's talk, I realized that the study of Kabbalah was still another example of this rule of opposites. For how long had traditional religion denied study of the *Zohar* to the average person? In fact, it wasn't until the time of Rabbi Yehuda Ashlag that the world was given access to Kabbalah. During his own lifetime, opposition to Kabbalah was so strong that Rabbi Ashlag was once physically beaten for studying it. Because of this extraordinary opposition, he knew, as did Rabbi Brandwein, that Kabbalah must surely be an important field of study. This is not to say that the study of the Talmud is not also important, because it is. But the fierce opposition to Kabbalah study served to highlight the deep need for it.

Today many people still refuse to study reincarnation, though the Ari wrote that unless people examine their past lives, they will never know how to correct themselves in the present one. Redemption will be beyond them, and they will be forced to reincarnate again and again. As it is written in *The Gate of Reincarnation*, "A man is the spirit that is within the body, and the body is only the garment of the man."

I frequently assured Rabbi Brandwein that I would take it upon myself to disseminate all aspects of Kabbalah, and I have attempted to do this to the best of my ability. Regardless of whether my endeavor leads to financial loss or any other kind of damage, I will in no way compromise this goal. It is really for this reason that, during all my years of promoting the study of Kabbalah, I never felt fear. Rabbi Brandwein promised that as long as I proceeded consistently toward my objective, I would be certain of victory, and I have never wavered in my belief in this.

ONLY A FOOL HITS AT THE STICK, INSTEAD OF THE ONE HOLDING IT

Rabbi Brandwein taught me to look at those who might hate me as simply messengers or tools of darkness. "If a person were attacking you with a stick," he would ask, "would you strike back at the stick, or at the person wielding it? It's the same with hatred. Darkness and negativity are the true forces behind all hatred, and we must concentrate every ounce of our attention on those sources, not on the messengers. In the meantime, the attacks we receive will help us achieve our *tikun*, our personal correction. The attackers will receive their payment, do not worry. Since all people have a choice whether or not to express hatred, their choice to do so is a sign that they have succumbed to the forces of darkness, and this can only diminish their own Light."

Rabbi Brandwein often spoke of these issues out of concern that people would one day attempt to stop me from my mission, as people had tried to stop him. They might even try to have me put in jail. "Do not forget, however, that no one can do you real harm," he would say. "The true purpose of their actions is to test your faith in the Light of the Creator. Will you conduct yourself as your enemies do, only believing in the Holy One when it is comfortable to do so, or are you in this struggle until the end? Believe me when I say that the more you can endure suffering and hatred, the greater your success will eventually be. If others only knew how much stronger their hatred makes us, they would certainly alter their actions."

In *Beresheet*, the first book of the *Torah*, it is written that, *"Sin crouches at the door."* We are tested because the Light of the Blessed One must determine whether we believe in the Laws of Creation. Are we truly prepared to restrict our reactive instincts? To merit the Light of The Creator, we must be without all negativity and darkness. When the Satan appears before us to beg for his portion of Light, we must gladly relinquish it to him. Fed for the time being, he will skulk back to his corner.

To the best of my ability, this is how I have conducted myself for the last 30 years. Because of this, my teacher's promises have all come true—every one of them. What revelations there have been! What initially appeared bad has been transformed to good. When we hate others and feel justified in our hatred, this is precisely in accord with the Satan's purposes. *By failing to restrict our impulses to strike back at our attackers, it is ourselves we hurt most. We deny ourselves Light, and instead give it to the Opponent.*

Rabbi Brandwein taught me to view every problem as a passing illusion. By the Light of The Creator, I can observe my own reactions; if I use self-restraint and act according to Universal law, darkness and negativity will eventually vanish, and I will be bathed in Light. The reverse, however, is also true. The Satan lurks everywhere.

By the mid-1970s, our stock of The Gate of Reincarnation was starting to run low and we began a second printing. I realized that the growing interest in reincarnation was due to our strong belief and commitment to our work. Regardless of the response of our enemies, we had held to our vision.

We did not react to those who would hate us. Slowly but surely, people who had wandered far from their spirituality were returning to The Creator.

THE BLOWS WE RECEIVE ARE EQUIVALENT TO GOLD

The problems we encounter in life are truly for our benefit. We rail against our troubles with self-pity and anger, but without adversity we could not receive the blessings of The Creator.

"One who seeks the spiritual path in life must not be afraid of pain," Rabbi Brandwein would say. He once told me a story to illustrate this point and to stress the idea that we should actually welcome difficulty.

This was nearing the end of my studies with him. More and more often, he would refer to the years that lay ahead for me. He predicted they would be difficult, at least for a time. I was always adamant in my belief that I would never leave his side, though perhaps I was also preparing myself for the inevitable. So I listened carefully to all his words.

"Adversity will be your friend, for without it The Creator has no way of testing your true faith. Do not shrink from the future," he said, "for through you The Creator will certainly achieve wonders."

He paused a moment. Outside children coming home from school were laughing in the courtyard, their young mothers chatting happily as they hung their laundry out to dry.

"I know a wonderful tale that illustrates this point perfectly," Rabbi Brandwein continued. "Have you ever heard the story of Moshkeh? When I was a child, our old Rabbi would often tell us this story, to explain what might lie ahead in our lives and why we should not be afraid."

I settled back in my chair to listen to the tale, for in addition to everything else Rabbi Brandwein was a wonderful storyteller.

"This takes place in Russia, probably a hundred years ago. As our Rabbi explained it, it was customary at that time for landlords of great estates to have a single Jewish man working for them, as a kind of deputy should the lord need to go away. On Moshkeh's estate, the landlord was a very handsome young gentleman. In preparation for his upcoming marriage he told Moshkeh he would be away for three weeks. Moshkeh would have complete authority over all the peasants and servants.

"Now Moshkeh was no longer a young man at

this point in his life, nor had he complete authority over anything for many years. Naturally, he was quite excited. The very first morning he took tea on the veranda of the great estate and imagined himself a wealthy lord, going to important functions and signing treaties. What a glorious life he would have! His son would be a rich man! His daughter would be well-married!"

"He soon found out, however, that managing the estate was no easy task. While the peasants followed his orders that first day, they soon became angry, and by nightfall, had gathered around Moshkeh and were beating him severely. After all, here was an old Jewish man telling them what to do. What other choice did they have?"

"One thing led to another, and this went on for the entire three weeks. Each morning, Moshkeh would appear, ready to take charge, and each evening his workers would beat him. By nightfall, he would go home badly bruised, with tears in his eyes. His wife was sympathetic, but there was nothing that could be done. They needed the money. She bathed his wounds, and the next day he received more."

"At last, the three weeks were up and the young landlord returned, full of excitement about his upcoming marriage. He was also quite happy about the condition of the estate. It was well-cared for and the peasants had been productive. When he invited Moshkeh for a cup of tea, he saw that he was bruised on all parts of his body. Naturally, the land-lord asked what had happened. Moshkeh explained, and the landlord ordered that Moshkeh be given one golden ruble from his own treasury for each blow he had received. Moshkeh had received many blows, so he was given a great deal of money."

"Moshkeh took the money but by the time he arrived home he was crying. His wife took one look at him and asked him, with a broken heart, if he had been beaten yet again."

"No," Moshkeh answered. "I have been given money…"

He unfolded his bundle, and hundreds of rubles feel on the table. "We shall never have to work again," he said, tears falling from his eyes.

"Then why, husband, are you crying?"

"Moshkeh shook his head and tried to dry his tears. 'It's these rubles,' he said, touching them light-ly. 'I am sad because I was not given twice or even three times the number of blows. If I had, just think the amount of money I would have. I would be a lord myself. Why did I not suffer more?"

Rabbi Brandwein stopped speaking and smiled. "This is the kind of attitude we all need to have regarding our problems in life," he said. Our troubles are *for our own benefit*. Like Moshkeh, we should ask for more."

ONE MUST NOT PLAY GAMES WITH HIS BLESSED LIGHT

Two students of Rabbi Yehuda Halevy Ashlag once had a disagreement concerning printing rights of certain Kabbalah books. Years went by and still they were unable to settle the matter. Most people close to the matter hoped the men could to come to terms between themselves and avoid going to court. Court cases do not belong to Kabbalah. One must not litigate over the Creator's Light.

Nevertheless, one of Rabbi Ashlag's students fell prey to his negativity and brought the other to court. A short time later, this man died in the middle of a legal hearing, and the other died a year later. It was immediately clear to all involved that the move for a legal solution had been a big mistake. Such actions are against the laws of Kabbalah.

This story relates to something that happened not long after the Rabbinit Karen and I had finished printing *The Gate of Reincarnation*. Rabbi Brandwein had now been gone from us for a few years, and we were continuing with his vision. One of Rabbi Brandwein's benefactors, who had helped him to publish the complete *Writings of the Ari*, suddenly showed up on our doorstep. In a very loud voice, he stated that the rights for printing all of *The Writings of the Ari*, including *The Gate of Reincarnation*, were his.

I was sure this wasn't so, but he was adamant. Naturally our lawyer immediately investigated his claim and found that it had no merit. Nevertheless, the man threatened to take us to court if we did not surrender all the volumes of *The Gate of Reincarnation* that we had printed so far.

I was unsure what to do, but I remembered the story of Rabbi Ashlag's students. I also thought of what Rabbi Brandwein would surely have said, "You mustn't ignore the good turn he has done you." Indeed there was a time when this man's financial aid had been instrumental in publishing my teacher's books. Financial problems had always been a major obstacle for Rabbi Brandwein, and without this man's aid, who knows if *The Writings of the Ari* could have been published at all? While the help had been extended to Rabbi Brandwein, I felt it had been given to me as well.

I did not want to go to court against this person, so I tried to reason with him. I reminded him that at one time, there had been no buyers for *The Writings of the Ari*, and that I had had to convince the Kabbalah Centre branch in the United States to buy the entire inventory. Although the man in question had once been wealthy, by the time the inventory was sold, he had no money left and the sale had surely been a help to him. Unfortunately, this person did not want to remember any of this. He felt anger against The Creator for the loss of his wealth. Finally, we gave him all the volumes of *The Gate of Reincarnation* without complaint or resistance, and we parted as friends.

A year to the day that we had given this man the books, he died of a heart attack. There was no warning; he simply passed away. His death caused me great pain because this man, who had once been Rabbi Brandwein's student, had not learned the most central lesson of Kabbalah: that we must honor and share the Light of The Creator. Just as the soul is a part of the supernal Omnipresence, so too is Kabbalah. To argue about the *Zohar* or any of the material of Kabbalah goes against all spiritual laws. Rabbi Brandwein warned me never to play games with the Light and never to seek the court's legal solutions, and I have followed his advice to this day.

One must do everything possible to avoid conflict. It is better to run from an issue, literally, than to engage in contentious legal debate. Yet obviously these rules have not touched those outsiders who believe that they can do as they please. They need to be made aware that they cannot go against Kabbalah simply because they are so inclined. For in the end, they will surely pay for the hatred they inflict on others.

THEY BOTH KNEW
MY INTENTIONS

Rabbi Brandwein read my thoughts so easily, as did his teacher Rabbi Ashlag. I am sure they both knew all along what my intentions were concerning the sacred mission which they had begun.

In one of his letters to me, Rabbi Brandwein warned me never to work with a certain student of Rabbi Ashlag's, not even to make an informal connection with him. This was at the beginning of my studies with Rabbi Brandwein, and I hardly understood what he meant. But since I had made a clear commitment to my studies, I decided I would try to follow his advice. I now know, however, that I did not take his advice seriously enough. Perhaps I was swayed by what I heard from others. I had heard, for example, this particular student had only good things to say concerning Rabbi Brandwein, and especially concerning the work my teacher was doing on the *Unpublished Fragments From the Zohar*, *The Tikunim of the Zohar*, and his commentary on the *Rungs of the Ladder*.

Many in our small community were also aware that this student had written about Rabbi Brandwein in glowing terms, clearly acknowledging the fact that Rabbi Brandwein had taken over the work of Rabbi Ashlag. Rabbi Ashlag's own two sons were Kabbalists, but were somehow unable to carry on the work, especially *The Tikunim of the Zohar*, *The Writings of the Ari*, and The *Ten Luminous Emanations*, which was Rabbi Ashlag's greatest achievement. Because Rabbi Brandwein was the only one who fully comprehended the importance of The *Ten Luminous Emanations*, he was the only one who could undertake its publication. That I had the privilege to study this work with Rabbi Brandwein in person, is something for which I will be eternally grateful.

I was puzzled by Rabbi Brandwein's advice against any contact with the student. At this time, I was living half the year in the United States, to earn my living and to help subsidize Rabbi Brandwein's academy, and I unfortunately ended up working with this person on a few English translations when

I was in New York. He lived in dire poverty. His only interest was the spread of Kabbalah and his family had abandoned him since they had no interest in his work. Witnessing his hardships, I ascribed them to the fact that the time was simply not yet ripe for Kabbalah to be widely disseminated, as it is today. What other reason could there be? When this man passed away, not a single person attended his funeral besides Rabbi Brandwein and myself—neither his wife nor his children. Rabbi Brandwein, who had stayed in touch with him after his move to the United States, took care of the funeral arrangements and paid for his burial plot.

Then, a few years ago, the man's son contacted me with a court order stating that he was his father's legitimate heir, and was suing me for stealing his father's books. You can imagine how astonished I was—not only by the son's completely false allegation, but even more so by the accuracy of my teacher's warning. Here, he had seen 30 years into the future and predicted the darkness that would follow this man through time. I can only thank The Creator that I did not work on more books with this student, and I owe this solely to Rabbi Brandwein's warning.

To this day I thank The Creator that Rabbi Brandwein's support and advice continue to help me, during his lifetime and beyond.

WHAT HAS TAKEN PLACE SO FAR IS LIKE A DROP IN THE OCEAN

Even before I met them, Rabbi Ashlag and Rabbi Brandwein had already determined that I would be the vessel through which they would manifest all of their intentions. Together we achieved so much! But soon such great events will occur that what has taken place so far will appear like a drop in the ocean.

Multitudes of people today know the word Kabbalah, and more multitudes have returned, in some form or other, to a deeper spirituality. To give just one small example, thousands of men and women today follow the tradition of *mikveh*, the ritual bath, and this was hardly true in the past. I certainly do not claim sole credit for this. It is obvious to me that the wonderful miracles that have taken place would not have been possible without the help of Rabbi Brandwein, and his teacher before him Rabbi Ashlag. They are helping me to this day to spread the word of Kabbalah—after their deaths even more than during their lifetimes.

Consider the power of the *mikveh*. Before I met Rabbi Brandwein I went to a *mikveh* daily, but the benefits were negligible in comparison to what I learned after I met him. Because of Rabbi Brandwein's guidance concerning this tradition, especially his advice for meditation and the timing of the immersion, I now understand its potential for healing the sick. Furthermore, the holy names that we now use in the *mikveh* came about only because of the teachings of Rabbi Brandwein and Rabbi Ashlag. Before them, we knew nothing. And this is also why revelation of the secrets of Kabbalah is now occurring much more quickly than in all the preceding 2,000 years. In the past, miracles were only performed by learned Kabbalists who had special access to the sacred tradition. Today, Kabbalah is available to everyone. People live and learn Kabbalah on a daily basis and experience its wonders as a part of their everyday lives.

Why did I receive this help from Rabbi Brandwein and Rabbi Ashlag? It seems incredible that for the past 30 years I have been the recipient of such great wisdom, yet without their intercession, how could so many wondrous events have taken place? In spite of all the accusations and insults that have been directed toward us, what we have achieved cannot be denied or made to disappear. The many people who have worked within this spiritual tradition should be proud of their actions and what they have achieved with us. This is another truth that cannot be denied. The ocean which we have all created is truly great.

THROUGH KABBALAH, WE TRANSCEND THE LIMITATIONS OF TIME

As the relationship between Rabbi Brandwein and myself grew stronger, I slowly began to manifest his intention of spreading the truth of Kabbalah to the world. Rabbi Brandwein's many books, which had been locked away in storage, now began to reach the general public. Of course, this delighted him. Perhaps I was chosen to help because of my business experience earlier in life; or perhaps there was another cause. I do not know the exact reason. Perhaps it was simply time for the teachings of Rabbi Brandwein and Rabbi Yehuda Halevy Ashlag, begun 50 years earlier, to finally reach the world.

When I first met Rabbi Brandwein, he was not at all concerned with the infinite details of life in the physical world. His thoughts were entirely given over to The Creator. Yet from his letters, one can see how great his vision truly was. For whatever reason, I was the student who most fully grasped his full intention, especially for promoting the study of Kabbalah.

It has taken decades to bring Rabbi Brandwein's vision to life, but now I can say that it has been accomplished, and it would not have been possible without Rabbi Ashlag and Rabbi Brandwein's great inspiration to manifest their teachings. There have been so many obstacles, not the least of which has been the hostility and jealousy from other religious groups. The hatred which we inflict on each other, the same hatred that brought about the destruction of the Holy Temple, continues to this day. To withstand this pain has been difficult and would not have been possible without my teachers' great love and example.

Rabbi Brandwein told me that in the future my only work would be bringing the study of Kabbalah to the entire world. What an extraordinary prediction! If someone besides him had said this, even ten years ago, I would never have believed it. I learned from Rabbi Brandwein, however, that all events and actions in life are connected to eternity. Time as we usually understand it does not exist. When we function within the Light of Kabbalah, we transcend the apparent limits of nature. Kabbalah literally makes the impossible possible.

I live within this amazing reality at every moment.

THE LIGHT OF THE BLESSED ONE TREATS US AS WE WOULD TREAT OTHERS

If people claim to be spiritual but hate others, they deny themselves the possibility of transformation and miracles cannot occur in their lives. That is why the Holy One, Blessed be He, sometimes chooses not to answer certain people's prayers, because underlying their faith is a hatred for others and this alone determines their fate. We must not assume that our prayers are unanswered if our lives do not take exactly the turns we want. Sometimes the answer is, "No!"

Many of Rabbi Brandwein's students and relatives spent years at his side, yet never grasped his central message nor the essence of his thought. Today, they express hatred towards me though fortunately this hatred is in vain. In spite of their ill will, I continue to remember my teacher's words: Ignore this kind of hatred and the Light of the Blessed One will cause wondrous events to occur, events you might even call miracles. I believe that the miracles that have blessed us over the last 30 years are a direct result of this piece of advice. We do not fear others and are guided only by our love for all people.

Rabbi Brandwein also taught that we must stay

constantly vigilant against the lures of the Satan, who works day and night. When a spiritual person falls prey to his temptations, it is pointless to ask the Light of the Blessed One for mercy. The Light deals with us exactly as we deal with others according to the principle, "As He is merciful, so should you be merciful."

Those who hate others will eventually get what they deserve. It is not for us to create their punishment.

THE GIFT OF THE THIRD MEAL

The *Zohar* predicted that in the time of the Messiah, "people in the world [would] wail and no one [would] pay attention. They [would] turn their heads to all directions and look for deliverance, but [would] not find a remedy for their predicaments."

The one hope of deliverance, the *Zohar* teaches us, is in the place where people study "an unblemished Torah scroll, inscribed with the name of the Holy One. When this scroll is taken out, all people will be awakened, even the very lowest among us. But woe to the generation whose Torah scroll is paraded in the streets for prayer, and there are no reawakenings, for this generation is surely lost. No prayers will be answered, because there has been no repentance or fasting. The world might be in great suffering and pain, with problems pressing from all sides, and this Torah scroll is needed more and more, yet not a single man or woman will be aroused to prayer."

I learned from Rabbi Brandwein that in our struggle for repentance, all aspects of our spirituality are necessary. For some reason, however, we neglect the most important aspects of our daily practice, and instead emphasize ones of lesser importance. How can this be? As the *Zohar* says, *"The Torah scroll will be paraded through the streets, yet none will see it or be called to prayer."*

Consider, for example, the third meal of Shabbat. According to Kabbalah, the third meal combines elements of the other two. It thus bestows the greatest blessings and fulfillment on us, more than the other two meals together. At this meal we can create a permanent connection with The Creator that will see us through the entire week to come. Unfortunately, this is the meal that most people make light of, or skip entirely. A snack perhaps, a few prayers—what more is needed at the end of a Shabbat?

This attitude is completely wrong. Similarly, in too many synagogues people leave as soon as the reading of the Torah begins or they start talking and chatting and visiting with their neighbors. It's as though the reading were some kind of signal for intermission. Many synagogues do not even make sure that their Torah scrolls are kosher to begin with.

Rabbi Brandwein emphasized the significance of every aspect of spiritual practice. It was important, he said, to go to the *mikveh* just before the Mincha prayer of Shabbat, and to also go to the third meal of Shabbat. Before studying with Rabbi Brandwein, I myself had never heard of the great healing power of the third meal, nor of its power to create a permanent connection with the Creator.

Even the songs bring us closer to The Creator. "Think of the song *'Yedid Nefesh,'*" Rabbi Brandwein would say. "What a beautiful melody and words: *'Glorious, resplendent One, Light of the world, my soul is lovesick for you; I beseech you, Oh G-d, pray heal her by showing it the sweetness of your splendor. At that moment the soul will be strengthened and healed and will experience everlasting joy.'*"

Rabbi Brandwein explained that the power of this song comes from the line, *"Oh G-d, pray heal her."* This line has great healing power but in order for this to take effect, we must learn to avail ourselves of all of the treasures that have been given to us by The Creator.

HIS FACE SHONE AS WITH
THE LIGHT OF THE SUN

On the last afternoon I saw Rabbi Brandwein alive, his face literally shone as with the light of the sun. In all the years I had known him, I had never seen him so radiant. I could feel in his presence, in the room around us, in everything we discussed, that he was ready to depart this world.

When I think of Rabbi Brandwein's death, I am always reminded of Passover, since he left the world he loved so much in the season of this festive holiday. During the seven years I studied with Rabbi Brandwein, I spent every Passover with him, and the year of his death was no different. That year, he had arranged for the Seder, or ritual meal, to be held in the Old City of Jerusalem. I can recall walking the winding streets of the ancient city with the calm anticipation I always felt before the Seder. I imagined the Seder table, and the burning candles, the prayers we would say together.

As I knocked on the old door of the dining room, Rabbi Brandwein himself came out to greet me. I sensed he was well, yet his face was suffused with a kind, gentle light. With an apologetic air, he asked me not to go inside.

"Why?" I asked. "What is wrong?" Of course I was shocked. For the first time since I'd met him, he was turning me away.

He gently explained that someone at the Seder table was against our being together, and he simply did not have the strength to fight any longer. I had known for quite a while that this person was very jealous of our closeness, yet I did not realize how deep that hatred was. I could see how sorry Rabbi Brandwein was about this situation and that he was very sad. I asked him not to worry and we embraced. By the time I left, we both had tears in our eyes.

The days of Passover continued, and in spite of the festivity of the holiday, I felt deep sadness. I said the prayers with my family, yet always in my mind I saw Rabbi Brandwein praying over his old candelabras, the glow of the light twinkling softly on his face. I felt that I should be at his side. Finally, I could resist no longer. On the Sunday of Passover week, I returned.

Unlike the first day, however, the house was now quiet and full of sadness. Evidently Rabbi Brandwein's condition had worsened and he was now bedridden. The man who had not wanted to see me was grieving in a back room. One of Rabbi Brandwein's assistants led me to his bedroom as he explained the problem. The doctor had prescribed pills for his heart condition, but since Rabbi Brandwein was unsure whether or not they were kosher, he was reluctant to take them. His illness had worsened quickly and now little could be done.

As soon as I entered the room, all I saw was his gentle face on its pillow, a warm yellow light streaming through the windows.

"Shalom, old friend," I said.

"Shalom," he answered softly.

We spoke quietly for a few minutes, but now my enemy in the house had learned of my presence and barged into the room angry and agitated. Rabbi Brandwein did not ask me to leave, but to keep the peace I said I would make a visit to the Western Wall and return later.

Out in the streets there was the usual hustle and bustle of Jerusalem—the young children, the shopkeepers, the tourists. This wonderful city distracted me from what I feared was coming. I strolled down the narrow streets contemplating all I had learned from Rabbi Brandwein, even imagining our future together when he would recover. This was a vain hope, of course, but I was not quite ready to face the truth.

Then, for some reason, I was seized with a terrible anxiety that a bomb was about to go off in the Jewish quarter. "I must return," I said. "I must get back as soon as possible." There was no rhyme or reason to my presentiment, yet I was sure something terrible was about to happen to Rabbi Brandwein, and that my only place was at his side.

Though it had only been an hour since I had left, when I returned to his bedroom, I found him in much worse condition. I had never seen him so weak or in such a state before, and at the same time his face shone as with the light of the sun. I could feel that he was about to depart this world.

I pulled a chair up close to his bed and stroked his soft brow. Though he was very weakened and it was clearly difficult for him to speak, we discussed many future events—things we had never before spoken of. At times, I had to bend to hear his voice, yet his thoughts were as clear as ever, and he spoke with a gentle directness, wanting me to grasp everything he had to tell me.

Finally, the doctor arrived. He said Rabbi Brandwein needed to go immediately to the hospital. Of course he did not want to, but we called the ambulance anyway. As it drove away, I wept, pleading with Rabbi Brandwein not to leave, not to abandon me in the difficult period that I knew lay ahead, but it was to no avail. He had already decided to leave this world.

The soul of my righteous teacher and Rabbi departed on the afternoon of that day, in the middle of Chol Hamoed, the festive week of Passover. He was only sixty-five years old. Because he died in Jerusalem, we wanted his funeral to be as soon as possible, but this turned out to be difficult to arrange.

First, there was the problem of finding a *mikveh* to wash him, as there was only one *mikveh* in the area for such purposes and it was already closed. Finally, we found a private bath and washed him there.

Next there was the problem of a burial site. Rabbi Brandwein already owned a burial plot, but we did not know if we should bury him there or near his own master Rabbi Yehuda Halevy Ashlag, who was interred in the Har Hamenuchot cemetery. I told the family that Rabbi Brandwein always sought to be near his teacher and, thanks be to The Creator, they accepted my advice. The burial took place so quickly that we did not even have time for an announcement. A few radio stations broadcast the place and time of the burial, but we did not think many people would show up, and we were correct. Only the family attended.

ONE MAN—A KABBALIST— CHANGED AN ENTIRE COUNTRY

My teacher of blessed memory left this world in the same manner that he lived—a modest man who sought neither honor or glory. And since he did not seek honor in his lifetime, he left this world without fanfare. When his death became known, the newspapers wrote briefly about his life and work and that was all.

The Kabbalistic understanding of death is quite complex. On the one hand, the *Zohar* is very emphatic about the possibility—no, the *inevitability*—of immortality. Beginning in the year 5760 (2000 by the Gregorian calendar), powerful energies will come into play that will culminate in the demise of death itself. As so often happens, here again is a convergence of Kabbalah and modern science, where genetic research holds the promise of revolutionizing medicine, eliminating many fatal diseases, and extending the average life span well beyond 100 years. All this without even mentioning the leading-edge research on cloning and the aging process of cells.

Along with this, however, the fact remains that people are dying every day just as they have always died. Even the great Kabbalists died. But Kabbalah teaches that people's deaths can be as different as their lives. For the great majority of human beings, death is something that simply happens to them. Whether out of fear, fatigue, or a sense of futility about their lives, they allow their lives to come to an end. Though this process often takes place outside conscious awareness, it's often very evident to family and friends. Physicians even have a term for this last act of renunciation. They refer to it as "turning your face to the wall."

For a Kabbalist, however, death is not an act of giving up or giving in. Instead, there may come a time when a great soul is ready to move on, having accomplished all that was needed in the physical realm. This is a positive choice, made with love for the world to be left behind and eagerness for the Upper Realms to be entered. This was the state in which Rabbi Brandwein experienced death, although I hesitate to even use the word "death" in this context. What took place was so fundamentally different from the way most people end their lives. To say of Rabbi Brandwein that he passed on was in no way a euphemism. I absolutely had the sense that his soul was ascending to another level of being, and one closer to G-d.

Other than his own teacher Rabbi Yehuda Ashlag, there has never been another Kabbalist to compare with Rabbi Brandwein. The books he wrote testify to his knowledge. Rabbi Brandwein often said that there were certainly many other Kabbalists in this world, and perhaps they were more righteous than he, but one had to look at their writings to judge their importance. The impact of both their writing and their actions in the world must be taken into account. From this perspective, there has been no greater Kabbalist than Rabbi Brandwein.

He changed the face of all of Israel, and with time it will be seen that he changed the entire world. The spreading of the study of Kabbalah could not have happened without the help of Rabbi Brandwein, my master, my teacher of righteous and blessed memory.

May his virtue protect us and all the nations of the world, Amen.